AF281006

Honeybuns

All Day Cook Book

Emma Goss-Custard

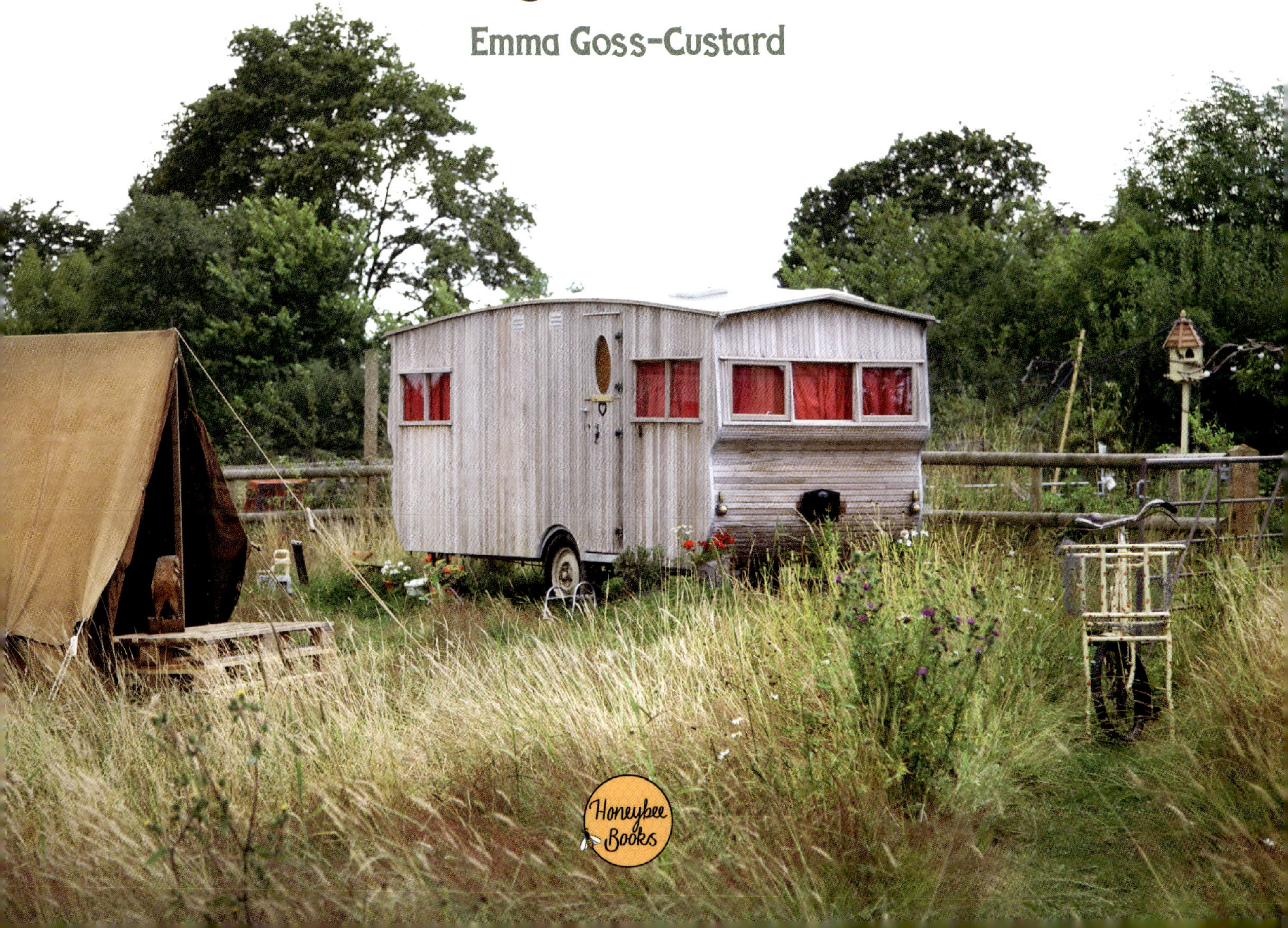

Honeybee Books

Published by Honeybee Books, Dorset
www.honeybeebooks.co.uk

Text Copyright © Emma Goss-Custard 2018
Design and layout © Honeybuns 2018
Photography © Honeybuns 2018

The right of Honeybuns to be identified as the owner of this work has been asserted by them in accordance with the Copyright, Designs and Patents Act 1988.

No part of this book may be reproduced in any form or by any electronic or mechanical means including information storage and retrieval systems without permission in writing from the copyright holders.

ISBN: 978-1-910616-45-1

This book is dedicated to Mog

Text: Emma Goss-Custard

Photography: Lucy Heath, except biog and introduction photographs of Emma by Katharine Davies Photography

Cover design: Sheree Evans at Sundown Studio

Design, layout and illustrations: Sheree Evans

Recipe contributors: Emma Goss-Custard, Margot Annelle Dimmer and Charlotte Drake-Smith

Styling and props: Lottie McMillan and Beverley Jones

Food styling: Bianca Nice

Proof readers: Luke Nelson, Peter Henshaw, Matt Goss-Custard, Kayleigh Taylor, Lottie McMillan and Emma Goss-Custard

Thanks to Beverley Jones, Lush Fabrics, Linda Browne and Georgie Matthews

Printed and Bound in India by Parksons Graphics

Emma Goss-Custard

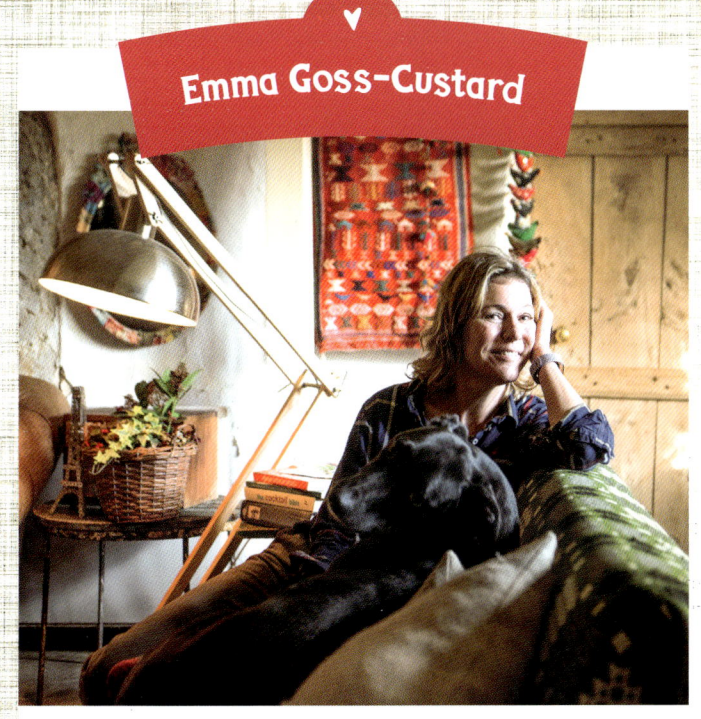

Margot Annelle Dimmer

Emma Goss-Custard started Honeybuns from a shared kitchen table in Oxford in 1998.

Emma, her husband Matt and their team now run the award winning bakery from Naish Farm in Dorset. Emma and Matt live in the farmhouse with their two small children and a beloved menagerie of rescue animals.

Honeybuns supplies a number of prestigious establishments in the UK from restaurant and coffee chains to airlines, and exports to the EU and further afield.

The bakery is gluten free and also produces vegan, dairy free and refined sugar free options. Honeybuns continuously endeavour to improve on everything they do and to create delicious and innovative cakes.

Honeybuns cakes and gifts are available to buy online at honeybuns.co.uk

Margot is a well respected, Dorset born and bred chef who has earned her place by working her way up through the ranks as chef and then head chef at prestigious hotels and event catering businesses in the area.

Margot is the chef proprietor of the popular Thyme after time cafe based at Spire Hill Farm, Stalbridge, DT10 2SG. Her husband Steve has now joined the business as it has flourished. Although outside catering (mostly on a supply only basis) is still a big part, the café now has become the mainstay.

Margot, although already well versed in allergies and intolerances, has used the time spent on this book to further her knowledge in both gluten and dairy free diets. She now offers an innovative range of "free from" dishes at the café.

Margot contributed practical help and creative input to this book.

Margot can be found at thymeaftertime.co.uk

Honeybuns

♡HOME MADE♡

MOG SAYS...

There's nothing better than digging up veggies straight from the garden and cooking a delicious fresh meal with them

Honeybuns

Emma Goss-Custard, founder of Honeybuns

Welcome to our second book!

Why gluten free?

Our background is in gluten free baking. When we established Honeybuns in 1998, we were pioneers of this new (to the UK) baking tradition. We've gained an extremely loyal coeliac following but it was originally the delicious alternatives to wheat flour including flax and ground almonds that first drew us to baking gluten free. We preferred baking with ground nuts and seeds due to their superior flavour, texture and moisture retention. The fact that they happened to also be safe for coeliacs was a very welcome added bonus.

Gluten free to us has never meant deprivation, rather it has opened up an ever expanding global buffet of alternative "free from" flours to experiment with.

Over **100** delicious recipes

Welcome to Honeybuns' second cook book. Listening to plentiful reader feedback on book one, this time round we've included lots of gorgeous savoury recipes to complement the sweet bakes which we've been making since 1998.

The savouries have been practiced and tweaked over the years and are enjoyed at our Honeybuns team "get together" meals throughout the year. I've also drawn from my personal favourites which we share with friends and family alike.

All of the recipes are gluten free and vegetarian which is where our original expertise lies. There are 69 dairy free and 35 vegan recipes to choose from. Dairy recipes are still represented and we include tips on how to convert recipes from dairy to dairy free. 84 of the recipes are nut free too.

Our challenge was to provide recipes which are inclusive to as many people as possible whilst still tasting deliciously decadent. Our gold standard would be for someone to not twig that a recipe was "free from" at all.

Honeybuns have had practical help and creative input from the fabulous Margot Annelle Dimmer from Thyme after time café in Dorset.

Butter

We've also enjoyed a long love affair with the butter dish. Just try one of our plain vanilla flapjacks to see how we love to bake with decadence. When Honeybuns started, we took the view that coeliacs and those opting to go gluten free also often craved an indulgent treat. Being coeliac doesn't mean you want to be good all the time. Hence the lashings of British butter in our original Honeybuns Classic Range of cakes.

New direction

It's also true that expectations of food's functionality and health giving benefits are evolving at an ever quickening rate. There is a growing groundswell of interest in plant based, dairy free and vegan foods which is driven by health, animal welfare and environmental concerns. Until recently, dairy free alternatives needed to be hunted out in health stores; now they've gone properly mainstream.

Sugar is also understandably under scrutiny right now. This put us in an interesting position as bakers of all things naughty and nice. Being a gluten free bakery, we cannot claim to offer any health benefits other than to those customers who cannot eat gluten. We have to be honest about the "treat" nature of our cakes. All of our cakes are relatively high in sugar, compared to other types of food. It matters little if the sugar used is a fruit paste, syrup or old fashioned white granulated. It's all sugar, albeit in various stages of refinement. We've set our stall in the "sweeteners" section of the store cupboard section (see page 16).

We needed to evolve as a bakery and start to provide much needed tasty dairy free, vegan, and nut free options alongside our beloved gluten free Classic Range. Thus our New Generation of cakes was introduced in 2017. We've extensively researched and trialled a plethora of dairy free, vegan and nut free ingredients to enable us to bake for those who need or choose to be free from additional allergens. At the same time we continue to recognise that many Honeybuns fans and readers of this book will still want dairy based recipes.

Variety all the way

The consistent message throughout the book is one of balance and choice. For instance, some days may call for a full on buttery blow out of a treat when the Dorsety Whirls (see page 79) would beckon temptingly. If you then want to ease off the dairy for a day or two, but still fancy a treat, the Jam Tarts (see page 75) might just swing it.

Excepting those who cannot tolerate certain foods or allergens, we do not advocate a permanent exclusion of any food. Nor are we promoting a specific health message beyond that of eating a balanced and varied diet where decadent treats are relished; just not every day.

Hopefully we manage to convey our love of bringing people together to share and delight in the food as well as the experience. We strive to be inclusive and to celebrate what we can eat rather than dwelling on what we can't.

The recipes

We wanted to provide a range of recipes from the very simple to those more adventurous ones which are best undertaken when time is not of the essence. With time being an increasingly rare commodity for many of us, we've included plenty of seasonings which can be made and frozen until needed. Seasonality has also been taken into account with the more summery recipes making the best of British soft fruits.

As well as the vegan and dairy free recipes offering up environmental and animal welfare advantages, they also prove to be economical too. Not having to spend on meat leaves more money to spend on high quality nut flours and the freshest vegetables.

All about Honeybuns

We're an artisan, gluten free bakery based in very rural Dorset.

The enterprise was started in 1998 in Oxford with me, an old post office bike and a shared student kitchen where those pioneering gluten free cakes were made. From delivering to delis and cafés by bike, we now supply to national customers including John Lewis, Leon Restaurants and Waitrose. We also supply from our online shop.

By commercial bakery standards we are still a small outfit, with 31 of us doing everything from baking and packing to marketing and new product development. We're often told that we represent a welcome change from expertly marketed food companies who don't make anything themselves. In this sense, we truly are the real deal and the original table top enterprise spirit continues to burn bright.

Our rural location and renovated old dairy buildings are home to the bakery. We are surrounded by a nature reserve in which we've planted hundreds of trees, hedgerow and bee friendly plants as part of our Bee Green initiative established in 2002. Being kind to our environment is part of our DNA.

Visitors are delighted to find that we are not on an industrial estate. For us, it's a huge compliment when people say, "it looks just like it does on the packaging and the website". Authenticity is our aim in everything we do.

Our beloved Bee Shack is the heart of the Honeybuns enterprise. In what was an old chicken shed, we have installed a test kitchen and cosy team room. The advantage of combining the two under one roof is that we get direct feedback from our team who can nibble on test kitchen offerings whilst on their tea breaks. If it doesn't pass muster at this stage then it's back to the mixing bowl for a rerun.

Find out more at honeybuns.co.uk

If asked what we're all about in a pithy phrase it would be "customer delight".

Availability of ingredients has improved enormously since we wrote our first gluten free cook book in 2012. This is mainly down to the growth of specialist online ingredient suppliers. Supermarkets have also upped their game and stock a surprisingly wide range of "free from" ingredients. For instance, supermarkets now regularly stock teff, sorghum and ground flax which you would previously have had to track down in specialist health food shops.

Please take a look at the listed suppliers at the end of this section for more help on where to go for what.

NB It's always advisable to carefully check the ingredients for allergens before you use them and if in any doubt refer to Coeliac UK at coeliac.org.uk. You can also try contacting the manufacturer directly.

It's not uncommon for manufacturers to reformulate recipes thereby altering the listed allergens.

Flours

The question we're most commonly asked is, "what flours should I use and once I've bought them how best do I use them?"

In an attempt to answer this we've carefully edited this vast array of flours down to focus on a delicious, versatile and obtainable collection of "go to" staples for your food cupboard. At the same time, we've included some more unusual options to try if you want to experiment a bit.

Here we class ground nuts, seeds, pulses and grains as flours.

Where we have had good results with an off the shelf gluten free flour we mention this under "Flour Swap" at the end of the recipe. This allows you to swap our chosen flours for an off the shelf blend if you prefer in that particular recipe. Doves Farm and Bob's Red Mill both do good all purpose flours.

Alternatively, our Honeybuns "go to" gluten free flour blend is one we make ourselves using 15% ground flax, 45% sorghum flour and 40% ground almonds. The recipes will work using this blend but not quite as well as the specifically listed flours.

At the end of the day, our philosophy is that if you're going to the trouble of making a lovely home made gluten free bread, cake or pastry, then it's worth investing in the right ingredients needed to get the best result.

A general tip on flours is that you can freeze them if you're concerned about using them before their best before dates are up. This is especially relevant to ground seeds and nuts which can become rancid if left exposed to the air for long periods.

In our first book, Honeybuns gluten free baking, we included a lot of ground nuts, namely ground almonds, hazelnuts and pistachios. We remain great fans as they give reliably tasty results as well as adding moisture and nutritional benefits to recipes. The downsides are their expense and the need for some nut free recipes to include those who can't tolerate them in their diet. At Honeybuns we benefit from being able to buy nuts in larger, more economical quantities. For home bakers having to buy in smaller, retail packets, this can be eye wateringly expensive. One option is to make your own nut flours by simply blitzing your chosen nuts, either skin on or off, in a food processor until you end up with a flour like consistency. You can then buy a large bag of whole nuts and make several batches of nut flour which you can then freeze. We've listed some suppliers who stock bulk sized bags of various ingredients at the end of this section.

This issue of expense has led us to discovering how versatile milled seeds are as an alternative to using ground nuts. In all the recipes, ground nuts of any variety are interchangeable with a milled seed blend, details of which are listed later.

Here we talk you through the flours we favour, why we like them and how to get the best out of them.

Almonds, ground

Almonds are one of nature's over achievers. Packed to the rafters with vitamin E and antioxidants as well as having cholesterol lowering properties to boot.

Their naturally occurring oils keep breads and cakes moist and their sweet flavour means you can add less sugar to recipes. You can use them solo, as per traditional Mediterranean style cakes, but you will get a denser result than if you blend them with sorghum flour or ground flax.

The almond bread (blended with flax) on page 35 is soft, moist, sliceable and utterly moreish. Almond based cakes, breads, cookies and pastries are all delicious and have great keeping qualities.

The downside is the price. Almonds are susceptible to drought and California, one of the largest growing areas, has been badly affected in recent years thus making them more expensive. The most cost effective way of buying almonds would be from a natural food wholesaler. Whole almonds are cheaper than ground and, as mentioned above, you can then make your own flour at home and freeze it. Alternatively you can use ground cashew or ground sunflower seed flour.

At Honeybuns we use around half a tonne of ground almonds each week and it's fair to say we've become quite intimately acquainted with their quirks and foibles. When they are harvested and what the weather conditions were whilst the almonds were growing affects their oil content. This we discovered when batches of our Amondi cookie appeared to be frying, rather than baking. This particular problem can be countered by adding a non-oily flour, such as sorghum, to mop up the excess oil. The key is to adapt the recipe if you encounter such variables.

Brown rice flour

This is easily available, relatively inexpensive and lends a crispness to pastry. We've used it in some of the savoury tart and quiche pastries where you want a bit of crispness. It is, like most gluten free pastries, quite fragile when you need to lift it and transfer to a tin. This is a non-issue as you can hand "squidge" the pastry into its tin without any drama.

We find it too heavy and drying to use on its own, so we blend it with either tapioca or cornflour. If it is used heavy handedly in a recipe, you can detect a slight grittiness in texture. Feel free to use white rice flour instead.

Chestnut flour

Chestnut flour is well used in France in chocolate based recipes. We've used this as a one-off in a bread roll recipe on page 161 where we combine it with mashed, roasted butternut squash. The resulting flavour is fantastic. Chestnut flour brings a touch of luxe and lots of moistness to bread and cake mixes. The snags are: it can be tricky to get hold of, it's expensive and it can be heavy or "claggy" if used on its own rather than blended. It's therefore best to mix it with sorghum and/or tapioca for fluffier, lighter results.

As a flavourful and more economical alternative try ground roasted peanuts instead.

Chickpea / gram flour

This is a valuable ingredient to include in baking owing to its nutritional benefits. It is 20% protein and contains high levels of vitamin A, B1, B2, niacin and vitamin C. It has a strong flavour and is a very heavy flour. We use it to add body and flavour to savoury pastry but only up to 25% of the flour blend.

Cornflour

This multi-tasking, neutrally flavoured flour can be used as a thickener and also blended with other flours to create a soft chewiness in baked goods.

If using it as a thickener, take care not to boil it as it won't survive anything over 96°C.

Golden flax, ground

Made from golden linseed; flax comes in two colours, brown and golden. To be honest, the only reason we favour the golden is that it looks more inviting when baked.

Nutritionally, flax is a great source of protein, fibre, omega-3 fatty acids and antioxidants. There is also good evidence for its blood pressure lowering qualities. There is an excellent UK grower and supplier, thelinseedfarm.co.uk, where you can buy flax and learn about its medicinal and culinary applications.

Baking with it is a delight. It lends a lovely wholemeal taste to breads and cake but without the heaviness. It is outstanding when used in biscuit bases for cheesecakes, as you'll discover when you get to the pudding chapter.

We use it in conjunction with other flours such as ground almond and sorghum. It can be bitter if you exceed more than 20% in any flour blend.

Hazelnuts, ground

This is a beautiful ingredient to use. Simple to blend in with other flours such as sorghum or polenta to make sweet tart bases, cookies and cakes. The flavour comes out strongly without you needing to use more than 50% ground hazelnut, in conjunction with other flours.

As with the ground almonds, you can make your own from whole hazelnuts to help make this ingredient less costly.

Hemp, shelled or hemp seeds

This interesting ingredient is available as a flour but it's the nutty tasting seeds we tend to add to flour blends for extra texture and flavour. Great to include in sweet and savoury bakes for those who can't eat nuts.

Nutritionally they deliver essential amino acids and contain an optimal balance of omega-6 and omega-3 fatty acids. We have used Linwoods branded shelled hemp.

Milled flaxseed, sunflower & pumpkin seed blend

This is one of our favourite flours. It blends easily with other flours and brings moisture, texture and layered flavour to sweet and savoury bakes. If you need to go nut free this is an excellent substitute and is nutritionally loaded with omega-3 fatty acids, vitamin E and fibre to name just a few.

Linwoods make a lovely blend and it's readily available either in the supermarkets or head to linwoodshealthfoods.com. Alternatively, try making your own by grinding and blending equal parts of each seed.

Polenta

This is dried, ground maize and is a rich golden yellow in colour. Flavour wise it's neutral. It creates a lovely, fluffy texture when blended with ground seeds or nuts. We use polenta this way in cakes and breads.

It also adds crunch to shortbreads and biscuits and can also be used instead of a bread crumb coating.

Quinoa flour

As with polenta, quinoa lends a lovely golden colour to baked products. Nutritionally it's an important flour to try and include in your diet as it's a complete source of protein, providing all the amino acids. Quinoa is also a good source of iron and antioxidants.

It's nutty in flavour and works well in both sweet and savoury recipes.

Sorghum / jowar flour

This is the best general purpose gluten free flour we've come across. It works brilliantly when mixed with moist nut and seed flours as it fluffs up and produces a soft eating cake. We use it happily in breads, pastry, cookies and cakes.

It's sometimes said it can have a slightly bitter after taste but we have had no problems using it up to 50% blended with ground almonds or a milled seed blend.

Nutritionally it's rich in vitamins and minerals. Specifically it's a good source of selenium and niacin, both of which have been cited as having possible anti-cancer properties.

Tapioca flour

Tapioca flour is one of our hardworking flours in the Honeybuns kitchen. It's virtually flavourless and lends body and chew to a recipe. It absorbs moisture and acts as a binding agent. You don't need very much. We blend it at 15% with sorghum and almond flour in sponge cake recipes.

Nuts & seeds

For those wanting to cook or bake for nut allergy sufferers it's important to be aware of certain misnomers and their potential for causing confusion. For instance, pine nuts are the edible seeds of the pine tree rather than tree nuts. According to Anaphylaxis Campaign UK's website it is highly unlikely a nut allergy sufferer would be adversely affected. However it would always best to check with nut allergy sufferers before you use them in a recipe.

Similarly, coconuts are not nuts but are botanically classified as a drupe. As with the pine nuts it would be advisable to check with the nut allergy sufferer that they're OK with them.

Whole seeds can be used instead of whole or chopped nuts in a recipe quite happily. Our "go to" seeds are: sunflower, pumpkin, pine nuts and golden linseed.

Where toasted nuts and seeds are called for, you can spread them out on a baking sheet and pop them in a preheated oven at 180°C / Gas 4 for 3-5 minutes. Seeds such as pine nuts, sunflower seeds and pumpkin seeds tend to take less time to toast. We start with 3 minutes and watch them like a hawk. You are aiming for a lightly toasted finish rather than a deep tan.

Nuts can be toasted for up to 5 minutes and we either leave them whole or roughly chop them, preferably with their skins on.

The alternative method is to dry roast them for the same amount of time in a frying pan on a high heat. You'll need to shake the pan around every 30 seconds or so.

We often add whole toasted seeds to pastry, bread and cake mixes for texture and a toasted, nutty flavour.

Once their packaging is open and they're exposed to air, seeds and nuts lose flavour and can become soft and rancid over time. Freezing them, either whole or in flour form, is a great option.

DAIRY & DAIRY FREE ALTERNATIVES

It's no secret that here at Honeybuns we've enjoyed a long term love affair with West Country butter. We use it extensively in our range of Honeybuns cakes for the delicious flavour it imparts as well as the creamy texture or "mouth feel" as we call it in the trade.

However, we have had more and more requests for dairy free products from our coeliac customers in particular. To quote from the Coeliac UK website, "Coeliac disease is a frequent cause of secondary lactose intolerance."

This inspired us to research more naturally dairy free and gluten free recipes for those who can't tolerate either. We were also keen to include a balance of dairy and non-dairy recipes for those just wanting to mix and match their intake.

Initially, we were sceptical as we'd been disappointed in the past with dairy free margarines and other butter substitutes we'd tried. Now we feel confident that the dairy free recipes we've developed here are every bit as delicious as their buttery cousins.

As befits our overall philosophy on food, we aim to make our food as inclusive as possible. For those with multiple allergies or none at all, we hope you will enjoy the many gluten, dairy and nut free recipes featured.

Any oil can be used instead of butter if you need to go dairy free.

So let's start with some dairy staples and some recommended dairy free alternatives...

Butter

Whenever we mention butter in a recipe we are referring to unsalted. This allows you to control the amount of salt you'd like to add. Generally in our recipes we call for the butter to be melted. This can be done easily in the microwave.

Go Dairy Free by substituting melted butter for a vegetable based oil such as rapeseed or refined coconut oil. Both of these are neutral in flavour and lend themselves to sweet and savoury baking. To replace solid butter we use a vegetable spread such as Pure or a nut butter.

Cheese

Care is needed to check that the cheese you buy is vegetarian. This is assuming that you would prefer the recipe to be totally vegetarian; if this is not the case then please ignore the following information.

Parmesan, Gorgonzola and Grana Padano cheeses are all made using animal rennet. Hence, when we refer to vegetarian Italian hard cheese we mean a parmesan style cheese made with non-animal rennet. Such cheeses are readily available in supermarkets. We love using Capricorn Goats Cheese which can be sliced and used to top various veggie dishes. It's approved by the Vegetarian Society.

Go Dairy Free by using the soy based brand Tofutti which is available either as plain cream cheese or with various herbs blended in. Available online and in health food shops. The plain version works well in sweet and savoury dishes. To be honest, we've not yet found a tasty dairy free hard cheese out there. We've therefore focused on including cheese free savoury recipes which don't rely on nasty cheese substitutes.

Cream

We use a variety of creams including crème fraiche, double, single and whipping cream.

Go Dairy Free by using a plain dairy free coconut yoghurt from Coyo. This works really well in a lot of recipes where you need a crème fraiche style consistency.

It's naturally dairy and gluten free and we use the plain version. It's great in cakes, breads and dips. Look out for it in supermarkets and health food shops. Use it instead of regular yoghurt, crème fraiche, sour cream or whipped cream.

In the book we detail how to create a whipped cream using chilled coconut cream. To offset the coconut flavour you can add a pure vanilla extract.

Milk

We use either semi-skimmed or full fat.

Go Dairy Free by using one of many plant based milks now available. We've had great results using soy, coconut and nut milks.

You can also use the following fats and oils which are naturally gluten free.

Avocado, fresh and oil

Fresh avocado can work well as a fat replacement in pastry crusts. It just needs mashing with a fork and blending with your other ingredients.

It can also work well in dressings as a replacement for mayonnaise or oil. We love blending it into dips for creamy textures. Please see page 148 for our avocado and chocolate ganache filled tart. Delish.

Avocado oil makes for a beautiful dressing for salads and roasted vegetables. Nutritionally it has everything going for it. The downside is the expense. You can always use one half rapeseed oil to one half avocado oil.

Nut and/or seed butters

Extremely easy to make by blitzing your chosen nuts or seeds in a food processor until a paste is formed. By toasting the nuts or seeds beforehand you'll enhance their flavour.

They will keep in the fridge or you can freeze them. Alternatively Meridian Foods do a great selection at meridianfoods.co.uk, and they're readily available. Works well for sweet and savoury dishes.

Rapeseed oil

This is the "go to" oil we prefer for sweet or savoury dairy free baking. It's neutral in flavour, has good binding properties in pastry and is affordable. There are lots of regional farmers producing and selling their own versions, so it's easy to buy local in this instance. Widely available in supermarkets, health food shops and online.

Refined coconut oil

This extremely versatile oil has a melting point of around 24°C. In the UK, owing to our temperate climate, it will usually be seen as a white solid substance rather than a liquid. Unlike unrefined or virgin coconut oil, the refined version does not have a coconut taste and is neutral in flavour.

We tend not to use it, as we prefer British rapeseed oil which we find has superior binding properties. However, for those who are Paleo, coconut is preferable.

Toasted sesame seed oil

Once only typically found in specialist Asian grocery stores, this lovely savoury oil is readily available in supermarkets. We use it in dressings and in stir fries. Not suitable for sweet dishes.

Unrefined coconut oil

We love using this when a pure coconut flavour is going to complement a recipe. As with the refined oil, it is typically seen in a solid, white state in the UK. In warmer climes it'll be liquid. If you are baking on a hot summer's day (we can dream...) be mindful that the solid oil will melt above 24°C so it might be prudent to refrigerate any baked goodies to avoid the oil oozing out. We use the Groovy Food Company organic extra virgin coconut oil but there are plenty of other brands out there to choose from. These are now stocked by some supermarkets as well as online and in health food shops.

Chocolate (dark, milk and white)

Although not a dairy product itself, chocolate either contains milk or may be cross contaminated. For safe dairy free chocolate we use Moo Free and Plamil. These are also registered vegan.

BEWARE INGREDIENTS WITH "HIDDEN GLUTEN"

We've collated below the ingredients in this book which can contain hidden gluten or traces of it. These are foods and ingredients you could reasonably assume would naturally be free from gluten. Often this is down to potential cross contamination during production or sometimes flavours like malted barley are used to add flavour. We've referred to gluten free brands that are readily available.

Baking powder

This used to commonly have flour added to it in the manufacturing process. Nowadays gluten free baking powders abound. We use Doves Farm.

It's a good idea to just use gluten free baking powder to lessen the chances of using the wrong one in a recipe. There is no difference at all in the performance of the standard and the gluten free versions.

Chocolate

If you are coeliac or gluten sensitive you do need to carefully check that the packaging states "gluten free". Commonly, chocolate is made on the same production lines as chocolate covered biscuits which contain gluten. It can be tricky to get manufacturers to declare their products as suitable for coeliacs. The brands we've used and have had good results with are: Moo Free, Noble Choice and Kinnerton. These are also dairy free.

Jams, chutneys and preserves

There's no clear reason why gluten would be added to any of these but labels are worth checking due to the risk of cross contamination in their manufacture. They could well be produced in a factory producing gluten containing sauces. The vast majority of brands will be fine, but it's always worth making sure.

Sausages, vegetarian

It's quite common to find that malted barley extract has been added as a flavour enhancer thus rendering them not gluten free. Quorn now produce good gluten free sausages.

Mince, vegetarian

We are delighted that Quorn have now brought out a gluten free range of the vegetarian meat substitutes. The veggie mince didn't used to be gluten free, again owing to the malted barley extract which they've now taken out. Be careful to check other brands' labels before using them.

Vegetable stock cubes or powder

Again there are lots of gluten free brands available now. We use either Kallo or Marigold cubes or powder.

Vinegars (and distilled grain based alcohol)

This is an area of some controversy. Some coeliacs who are extremely sensitive have reported feeling unwell after eating certain grain based vinegars. Although the manufacturers can prove that there is less than 20 parts per million of gluten present after the distillation process, there are many coeliacs and gluten sensitive consumers who prefer to only use non-grain based vinegars.

We've therefore just included balsamic vinegar or white wine vinegar in our recipes to avoid confusion.

Worcestershire sauce, vegetarian

Some brands can contain gluten in the malt vinegar used. We used the vegetarian, vegan and gluten free one from Biona which you can get in most healthfood shops.

Standard, non-vegetarian Worcestershire sauce contains anchovy paste.

A note about eggs

Whenever we refer to eggs in a recipe, we recommend using large, free range eggs.

In the Funky Monkey Cheesecake (see page 151) we recommend using pasteurised liquid egg white as the cheesecake is not baked. Pasteurised liquid egg white is the safe alternative to using raw egg white and it's now commonly available in supermarkets.

For vegans we've included naturally egg free recipes as we were not happy with the results and availability of the egg replacers on the market at the time of writing this book.

In the Honeybuns commercial bakery we are using an algae based egg replacer in powdered form which works well in some recipes. It is not however readily available to the consumer in the UK and is also extremely expensive.

Other options such as the liquid from chickpeas (known as aquafaba), and flax eggs have only yielded us mediocre results. Hopefully the algae powder will start to become more readily available by the time we write our next book.

A note about herbs

There is no substitute for fresh herbs. Personally I really do not like the taste of many dried versions especially dried thyme and basil which I find simultaneously musty and overpowering. Buying them in supermarket packets can be prohibitive and wasteful if you only need a snip of them in a recipe. I'd highly recommend growing your own on a windowsill or an outside pot.

This warrants an entire chapter of its own as it's a complex and highly emotive issue at the time of writing.

With obesity levels rising and the NHS already under great pressure, our sugar intake is understandably being scrutinised. At Honeybuns we recognise that eating sugar in excess is unhealthy whilst at the same time we appreciate the various functions that sugar performs in a recipe. To quote an article we've written and published on our own website:

"Aside from being highly palatable, sugar also performs other functions in baking including caramelisation, structure, and preservation. To replace it with another single "magic bullet" ingredient is not realistic. So it was off to the Honeybuns test kitchen for two years trialling a wide range of potential alternatives to added sugar".

We've attempted to strike an achievable balance between using a blend of processed sugars and other natural sources of sweetness such as fruit pastes and syrups. Sometimes nothing else will work as well as a full flavoured demerara or muscovado and in other instances a date paste would work just as well.

Certain types of sugar work best in certain recipes. For instance, sponge cake made using just fruit paste is going to be dense and stodgy in texture. Using a crystallised sugar such as demerara adds structure to the sponge as well as sweetness. There is no simple sugar replacer that will work brilliantly in all recipes. It simply doesn't exist. In baked treats, where the sugar is doing more than tasting sweet, we'd rather have a smaller slice of something than compromise on enjoyment. We are in favour, however, of reducing or avoiding altogether the added sugars in savoury dishes where the only function is to add sweetness.

Zero calorie sweeteners such as stevia, xylitol and erythritol are gaining popularity but are not suitable for using on their own in our sweet bakery recipes. They add sweetness but do not provide structure or caramelised finishes to baked products. They can work well in icings and toppings but this is not something we have explored in this book.

There is plenty of talk of healthier sugars and sweeteners on the internet and by many high profile food celebrities. One oft-voiced opinion is that unrefined sugars are healthier than refined ones. Certain sugars then come into vogue and are touted as healthier. We're of the opinion that all sugars need to be eaten in moderation. The research we've done by reading, baking and attending seminars leads us to conclude that sugar, be it naturally occurring fruit sugars or plain white granulated, needs to be consumed as a treat and in moderation. It's not the most interesting or on trend message to espouse but we feel it's truthful and practical.

Throughout the book we've referred to liquid and crystallised sweeteners of choice.

Please see the list below for our recommended interchangeable crystallised and liquid sweeteners. They do not all taste exactly the same, for instance light muscovado is richer in flavour than refined white sugar, but they will each give you good results in the more adaptable recipes. Where a specific sweetener works best, we'll specify it in the recipe, otherwise we leave it to you to select your favourites.

List 1 is a selection of interchangeable crystallised sweeteners. List 2 is a selection of interchangeable liquid sweeteners.

1. Interchangeable crystallised sweeteners:

Granulated white sugar
No depth of flavour but provides sweetness, structure and caramelising properties.

Demerara
A lovely, light caramel flavoured sugar providing sweetness, structure and caramelising properties.

Light muscovado
Please see demerara above, but with a richer, slightly burnt toffee flavour.

Coconut sugar
We don't find it as sweet as regular white sugar...but this can be seen as a good thing. Also it doesn't caramelise as well as the other crystallised sugars listed here.

2. Interchangable liquid sweeteners:

Golden syrup
A straightforward sweetener, great added to flapjacks and cookies for a moist yet chewy texture.

Honey
Can be beautifully flavoured depending on the variety. Intensely sweet and can burn more readily so you may need to keep a closer eye on cakes whilst they are baking and adjust the baking time accordingly.

Coconut syrup
Not as good at binding and adding chew as golden syrup but can work well in puddings and certain other recipes.

Date syrup
Good to use as a binder and a sweetener, the flavour is intensely datey though. Use if you're happy with the stronger flavour.

Agave syrup
Good for sweetness. We find that it doesn't bind and provide as much stickiness as some of the other options.

TIPS

Below is a collection of tips which are intended to help you along the way to making the most of the recipes with the least amount of guesswork or stress. As for the kit or equipment you need, we've attempted to keep this as simple and accessible as possible.

Read the recipe before you start

This may sound beyond obvious, but it really does help to read and re-read the recipe to enable you to collate kit and ingredients before you get your hands covered in cake mixture.

Preheat the oven (and learn its quirks)

Again this is not meant to patronise, rather to reassure you that we still sometimes forget to do this! It really will hamper your efforts if the oven is not fully up to temperature. Baking is quite an exact discipline and your oven will also have its own quirks to get used to. Try starting out with more forgiving recipes such as Super Easy Roasted Vegetables (see page 119) before attempting more complicated recipes.

Please note that all our recipes were tested in a fan assisted electric oven and all ovens will vary.

Melting butter

The best way is to pop it in the microwave for 30 second bursts on medium power. As with chocolate, it's quite easy to burn and there's no reversing this.

The important thing to remember with melted butter is to allow it to cool slightly before you add it to your other ingredients. Try not to add it directly onto raw eggs, lest you inadvertently scramble them. This would be a non-optimal outcome.

Melting chocolate

Again, the easiest way is to place the chocolate in a microwavable bowl and heat for 30 second bursts on medium power. After each 30 seconds, stir the chocolate to help melt it further. It's much better to carry on stirring to get rid of the lumps if it's close to being fully melted. If you overheat the chocolate there's no way of rescuing it. Instead it gets gritty burnt bits in it and turns everything bitter.

As a guide, 100g of chocolate takes 2 minutes to melt, in 30 second bursts on medium power.

Testing when a cake is done

There are a number of ways you can check this. You can use a cake skewer to insert into the middle of the cake and push it down well inside the cake. It should come out cleanly with no stodgy mix sticking to it.

The top of the cake should be domed, springy to the touch and a dark golden to mid brown colour. If your cake is browning too quickly in the oven you can place some baking parchment over the top of the cake to stop it burning. If it's a fan assisted oven you may need to use a larger piece of paper and tuck it under the bottom of the tin to prevent it from being blown about.

TIPS

To avoid air bubbles in cake and bread

Once you've poured your mixture into its tin, tap it firmly on a work surface to remove any trapped air bubbles which could then cause annoying craters and hollows once baked.

Cooling

We recommend using a wire cooling rack. To prevent your precious bakes from sticking to the wire rack as they cool, place baking parchment on top of the rack first.

Using frozen fruit and vegetables

We're great advocates of freezing leftover seasonal fruits and vegetables which can then be added to cakes and breads. Don't be tempted to save time by adding them in their frozen state to your mixture. This will freeze up your cake or bread mix and your bake will not rise. Any frozen additions need to be fully defrosted first.

Freezing saves time and faff

In the Crackers, Dips and Flavour Blends chapter (see page 178) there are lots of really handy recipes for sauces and flavour blends including chai spice as well as pastes like the punchy lemon and garlic one. These can all be frozen ahead of time and then defrosted when you need them. For pastes and liquids, freezing in an ice cube tray is a handy solution. You can also toast large batches of nuts and seeds and freeze these in readiness for a baking day.

Eggs

There is no need to keep your eggs refrigerated. They are safe at ambient temperature as long as you use them within their "use by" dates. They need to be at room temperature for baking. It takes 3 minutes to whip egg whites into stiff peaks.

KIT

Baking parchment

It's also called silicone paper and is coated with non-stick silicone. It's now widely available in supermarkets and out performs standard greaseproof paper.

Electric mixer

We deliberately left this open ended as you can use either a stand mixer or a hand held electric mixer in our recipes.

Stand (or sometimes known as a planetary) mixer. These mixers come with their own bowl and set of attachments. For all our recipes, except where whisking is specified, the beater attachment will work well.

Well known brands such as Kenwood and Kitchen Aid routinely get good reviews.

Electric hand mixer

We used a cheap as chips one for all the recipes that required mixing, and we didn't use the stand mixer at all, thus proving you don't always need to invest in the more expensive kit to get really good results. It's handy to have a good stock of lightweight plastic mixing bowls as well as a bendy silicone spatula to get all the mixture out from the mixing bowl.

Food processor

We used this extensively for the book recipes and it's also the reliable work horse in the Honeybuns test kitchen. Suitable for blitzing anything from batches of toasted nuts to a tapenade. It's always a good idea to stop during your blitzing to scrape down the sides of the bowl with a silicon spatula to ensure everything gets adequately chopped and mixed. If you were to invest in anything, then we'd recommend buying a food processor.

Tins, loaf

Depending on the recipe, we've used either 450g or 900g tins which is how they are commonly referred to. You can get them from Lakeland, Amazon and eBay amongst others. You can buy loaf tin liners in either size too if you'd rather not have the fiddle of cutting baking parchment to size. We prefer the cheaper, thin walled loaf tins which speed up the process of baking hefty loaves.

Tins, traybake

Where we've referred to a "traybake" we used a Mary Berry traybake tin available from Lakeland at lakeland.co.uk. The external dimensions are 34.5 x 24 x 4cm. You get 12 or 15 portions depending on how you cut it.

Other traybake tins are available, we just selected this as it's readily available.

Tins, round

Again, spring form and loose bottomed tins are readily available. These make the turning out of your cakes so much easier.

Baking sheets

These are ideal for baking cookies, free form pizza bases and breads. You just need to line them with baking parchment first. The standard size is around 37 x 35cm.

Muffin pan

We use a 12 hole silicone one and we'd generally recommend using paper cases as well, just to make turning out totally stress free. You'll need to pop anything silicone onto a metal baking sheet for stability.

Microwave

It's not essential as you can always melt butter in a pan on the hob and chocolate can be melted using the Bains Marie method instead...but....they are really handy. Ours isn't a fancy model. The key is to get used to the power settings beforehand. As previously mentioned in this book, once chocolate or butter have burnt, there's no reversing it.

Wire cooling rack

Again, there is no need to get anything fancy. The benefit to buying a cheaper version is that they're super lightweight and portable.

SUPPLIERS

Here are some of our "go to" suppliers for harder to find, specialised free from ingredients. We've chosen ones who supply to the public, not just trade.

Goodness Direct offer a great range of eco, organic and "free from" foods and ingredients.
goodnessdirect.co.uk

Doves Farm produce a lovely and extensive range of gluten free flours. We used their general purpose self-raising flour in some recipes with good results. Please look out for our "flour swap" tips where we suggest using Doves Farm.
dovesfarm.co.uk

Linwoods produce a fantastic range of ground seed mixes which can be used instead of ground nuts. Their blends often have many health benefits which are clearly labelled on the pack. You can't buy directly from their own website but they list their stockists including Holland and Barrett, Tesco and Ocado.
linwoodshealthfoods.com

Sous Chef sell a great range of harder to source international ingredients. They also carry a thoughtfully selected range of baking equipment.
souschef.co.uk

Bob's Red Mill Flours are of great quality and the range is broad. They specialise in gluten free and they're milled in the US. They're stocked by Healthy Supplies, as below.

Healthy Supplies are great at wholefood ingredients including superfoods and dried fruits. Their no frills website is clearly laid out, making it easy to locate store cupboard essentials.
healthysupplies.co.uk

Vicki Montague created a lovely wheat free and gluten free flour. Her blog is ranked on foodies100.co.uk.
freefromfairy.com

For really interesting natural flavourings and flours do check out Steenbergs.
steenbergs.co.uk

BREAKFAST
BONANZA

Eggs, muffins, waffles & toast

The freshest of eggs
for me and *you*,
when only the best breakfast
will cockadoodle-doooo

THIS EGG
BELONGS
TO POSH

Our wonderful
bantams Posh,
Pecks and Elton
are free to roam
the fields of the
Honeybuns Bakery

DELICIOUS

Crunchy Topped Breakfast Pots

SERVES 2
FREE FROM GLUTEN / NUTS

Served in tall glasses, this is a very pretty way to start the day. The raspberry pesto can be made in advance and stored for up to 5 days in the fridge. You can use any soft fruits rather than raspberries, if you prefer.

Pitstops

20g pumpkin seeds, toasted

25g sunflower seeds, toasted

15g pine nuts, toasted

20g crystallised sweetener of choice

4 tsp liquid sweetener of choice

¼ tsp salt

Breakfast Pots

2 peaches, pitted and cut into chunks

2 tbsp liquid sweetener of choice,
plus extra for drizzling

12 black or green grapes, cut in half lengthways

Finishing

Batch of Raspberry Pesto (see page 181)

250g Greek yoghurt

2 tbsp Florentine Mix (see page 186)

A handful of toasted coconut flakes

Preheat the oven to 200°C / Gas 6.

To make the pitstops, place all of the ingredients in a food processor and blitz for 1-2 minutes. The mixture is ready when it binds together when squeezed in your hand. Roll the dough out as thin as you can manage between 2 sheets of baking parchment. Peel the top layer of paper off and transfer the lower sheet with the rolled out dough onto a baking sheet. Bake in the oven for 4-6 minutes until the dough turns golden. Once out of the oven, leave on the baking sheet for a couple of minutes, and then transfer to a rack. Once cooled, cut into triangles and set aside ready to assemble. Any spare pitstops can be stored for a week in an airtight container or frozen.

Place the peaches in a roasting tin, skin side down. Drizzle all over with the liquid sweetener. Roast the peaches for 10 minutes, add the grapes, shaking the tin gently to coat them in the syrup. Roast for a further 5-10 minutes or until soft and at the point of collapsing. Once out of the oven allow to cool. The cooking time may vary according to the ripeness of the fruit.

Fill your 2 serving glasses with layers of the Raspberry Pesto, roasted peaches and Greek yoghurt. Sprinkle with the Florentine Mix and toasted coconut flakes and finish with a drizzle of liquid sweetener and pitstop triangles.

Eat on the day

TIP

Try adding some gluten free oats to the Greek yoghurt for more of a Bircher texture

Apple & Parsnip Muffins

MAKES 12 MUFFINS
FREE FROM GLUTEN / DAIRY / NUTS

These are best eaten warm from the oven. They taste too yummy to be virtuous, but just check out the ingredients. They're a veritable Spring clean in muffin form.

Topping

150g parsnip, grated
2 tbsp pumpkin seeds, toasted
85g liquid sweetener of choice

Muffins

85g polenta
75g milled flaxseed, sunflower and pumpkin seed blend
50g sorghum flour
1½ tsp gluten free baking powder
½ tsp bicarbonate of soda
1 tsp mixed spice, or use the Chai Spice (see page 185)
100g apple, grated
100g parsnip, grated
100ml rapeseed oil
100g liquid sweetener of choice
2 eggs
100g dairy free coconut yoghurt
3 tbsp plant-based milk

Preheat the oven to 180°C / Gas 4.

Line a 12 hole muffin pan with paper muffin cases.

Mix the topping ingredients in a bowl and set to one side.

Place the polenta, milled seeds, sorghum flour, baking powder, bicarbonate of soda, spice, apple and parsnip into a bowl and combine with a fork.

Put the oil, liquid sweetener, eggs, yoghurt and milk into another large bowl and beat with an electric mixer on high speed for 1 minute until the ingredients are combined.

Add the dry ingredients to the wet, and mix with a rubber spatula until all the ingredients are combined.

Spoon the mixture into the muffin cases, filling to nearly the top, then divide the topping equally amongst the muffins. Bake for 18-20 minutes until gently domed and springy to the touch. If baking without the topping then bake for 12-14 minutes.

Leave for 2-3 minutes, before carefully turning them out onto a rack to cool.

Omit the polenta, milled seed blend, sorghum flour, baking powder and bicarbonate of soda and replace with 200g gluten free self-raising flour.

Flour swap

Best eaten warm on the day. Can be frozen

TIP
Delicious using grated carrot or butternut squash instead of the parsnip

Big Breakfast Wraps

MAKES 2 WRAPS
FREE FROM GLUTEN / NUTS

A fully loaded wrap, perfect for those slightly "worse for wear" Sunday mornings when you need nourishment, tea and TLC.

Wraps

225g vegetarian mozzarella

2 eggs

115g vegetarian cream cheese

115g sorghum flour

100g fresh spinach leaves

50g vegetarian Italian hard cheese, grated

Sweet potato filling

400g sweet potato, peeled and grated

70g butter, melted

½ tsp cracked black pepper

1 tsp fresh thyme, chopped

Buttery mushrooms

25g butter

200g button mushrooms

½ tsp cracked black pepper

Finishing

Batch of Charlotte's Tomato Sauce (see page 194)

Best eaten warm from the pan

You can swap the sweet potato for butternut squash or carrot if you prefer

Preheat the oven to 200°C / Gas 6.

Line 2 large square baking sheets with baking parchment.

Place all the wrap ingredients in a food processor and blitz for 1 minute or until a paste is formed, then set aside.

For the sweet potato filling, start by placing the sweet potato, melted butter, pepper and thyme into a bowl and mix with a spatula. Then place the mixture in a roasting tin. Flatten the mixture down using a wooden spoon and bake in the oven for approximately 25 minutes or until the outer edges start to caramelise. Once cooked, remove from the oven and cover with foil to keep warm.

Evenly divide the wrap mixture between the 2 baking sheets. Using a palette knife, spread each dollop of wrap mixture as thinly as you can into 2 discs. Place both wraps into the oven for 7-8 minutes or until set and cooked through. They should still be soft and pliable.

Whilst the wraps are cooking, place the butter for the mushrooms in the frying pan; add the mushrooms and pepper and fry on a high heat shaking the pan regularly to coat them on each side. Cook for approximately 6-8 minutes then remove from the heat and cover with foil to keep warm.

Allow the wraps to cool slightly on the baking parchment. Using a palette knife, spread some of the tomato sauce through the centre of each wrap and spoon some of the sweet potato and mushrooms on top of the sauce. Lift the baking parchment to roll the wrap up so that the filling is enclosed in the middle. Either cut in half or into thick slices and eat whilst warm.

Chai Waffles with Caramelised Pears

MAKES 18 FINGER SHAPED WAFFLES
FREE FROM GLUTEN / NUTS
WAFFLES FREE FROM DAIRY

These lovelies are easy to make and turn out pleasingly light and fluffy. Don't stray from the batter recipe though. We tried making them with shop bought gluten free flour but they were not a patch on these.

Caramelised pears

40g butter

4 pears, peeled, cored and sliced (Conference or Comice)

2 tbsp crystallised sweetener of choice

1 tsp vanilla paste

½ tsp ground cinnamon

Finely grated zest of 1 lemon

Waffles

2 eggs

100g polenta

75g sorghum flour

100g tapioca flour

350ml coconut milk

75ml rapeseed oil, plus extra for brushing

4 tbsp crystallised sweetener of choice

1½ tsp Chai Spice (see page 185)

1 tsp gluten free baking powder

To make the caramelised pears, melt 1 tablespoon of butter in a frying pan on a medium heat. Add the pear slices and fry on each side for 3-4 minutes until golden brown. Remove the pears from the pan and set to one side. Add the sweetener, remaining butter, vanilla paste and cinnamon to the warm pan, place on a medium heat and stir until melted. Return the pear slices to the pan, turn them so that they are coated in the sauce and add the lemon zest. Transfer the mixture to an oven dish and keep warm.

Switch on your waffle maker to preheat.

Place all of the waffle ingredients into a bowl and beat with an electric mixer on high speed for 1 minute. Spray or brush the inside of the heated waffle maker with rapeseed oil. Start making your waffles by spooning the mix into your machine and cook for 3-4 minutes or until golden brown and crispy on the outside. Once cooked, stack your waffles on a plate and keep warm by covering with foil.

Serve the caramelised pears on top of the warm waffles.

Eat straight away

TIP

A light dusting of cinnamon on top of the pears is a lovely addition, as is a dollop of crème fraiche

IF YOU MAKE THE
BREAD SLIGHTLY THINNER
IT WORKS WELL AS A
RUSTIC PIZZA BASE

Herby Fried Egg on Triangle Toasties with Charlotte's Tomato Sauce

MAKES 12 TOASTIES
FREE FROM GLUTEN / DAIRY / NUTS

You can pimp this bread up ad infinitum. Pitted black olives work really well added to the dough. We also love the sweeter combination of chopped hazelnuts, raisins and rosemary... just omit the garlic listed here. If you spread the dough thinner you can create wonderful rustic pizza bases which you can bake off and freeze in readiness for a box set binge session.

Toasties

6 egg whites

100g tapioca flour

140g milled flaxseed, sunflower and pumpkin seed blend

90g ground golden flaxseed

2 tsp gluten free baking powder

3 garlic cloves, finely chopped

¼ tsp of sea salt, plus extra for sprinkling

½ tsp bicarbonate of soda

180ml coconut milk

50ml olive oil, plus extra for drizzling

1 large sprig of fresh rosemary, leaves taken off and finely chopped, or 1 tsp dried rosemary

Herby eggs (per person)

½ tsp fresh herbs, chopped (we used parsley and thyme)

⅛ tsp salt

⅛ tsp cracked black pepper

½ tbsp rapeseed oil, for frying

1 egg

Finishing

Batch of Charlotte's Tomato Sauce (see page 194)

Preheat the oven to 170°C / Gas 3.

Line a baking sheet with baking parchment.

To make the toasties, whisk the egg whites with an electric mixer on high speed until stiff peaks form. Pop the tapioca, milled seeds, golden flaxseed, baking powder, garlic, salt and bicarbonate of soda into a bowl and sift with a fork. Add the coconut milk and the 50ml of olive oil and beat with an electric mixer on high speed for 1 minute. Using a large metal spoon, gently fold a large spoonful at a time of the egg whites into this mixture, folding them in carefully so that you do not knock out the air you have whisked into the whites. You should end up with a smooth, fairly thick mixture.

Place the dough on the baking sheet and spread evenly with a palette knife to form a 20cm diameter circle.

Liberally drizzle olive oil over the top of the dough and push in with your fingertips, leaving indentations. Sprinkle with sea salt and the chopped fresh rosemary.

Bake for 20 minutes until golden and firm to the touch. Leave on the baking sheet for a couple of minutes, and then transfer to a rack. Once cooled, cut the round bread into 6 triangles then split each triangle in half lengthways. Toast these pieces either by putting them in a toaster, or placing the pieces on a baking sheet and putting them under the grill until they are golden brown. Once toasted, keep warm by covering with foil.

For the herby eggs, mix the herbs and seasoning in a bowl. We've listed the approximate amounts you'll need per egg. Just multiply up according to how many eggs you're going to cook. Warm the rapeseed oil in a frying pan on a high heat, crack in an egg, and sprinkle the herbs and seasoning over the yolk before the egg fully sets. We opted for a runny yolk. Cook a maximum of 2 eggs at a time, so you don't overcrowd the pan.

Next, spread a reassuringly thick layer of the tomato sauce onto each triangle toastie. Top with a herby egg and serve immediately. These look great on a big oval platter if serving for a group of friends.

The bread will keep in an airtight container for 3 days; reheat gently before eating to freshen up. Can be frozen

TIP

You can beat the spare egg yolks, adding ¼ tsp salt, then divide into small lidded pots and freeze. You can then defrost, add milk and use as a glaze for future baked masterpieces

Weekend Brunch Bake

MAKES 1 TRAYBAKE
FREE FROM GLUTEN / DAIRY / NUTS

This is super swift to put together and perfect for laid back weekend munchies. The vegetables we've used are a movable feast, so feel free to use whatever you have to hand. A cracking combination to try is garlicky mushrooms, fresh tarragon and black olives.

HOORAY IT'S THE WEEKEND

EGGSCELLENT NEWS

NAISH FARM

PYO

Vegetables

2 courgettes, thinly sliced lengthways

2 red onions, chunky slices

10 cherry tomatoes, halved

1 tbsp olive oil

½ tsp salt

1 tbsp fresh thyme, chopped

1 tsp cracked black pepper

1 tbsp gluten free soy sauce

Batter

150ml olive oil, plus extra for brushing

150ml coconut milk

3 eggs

100g polenta

55g sorghum flour

55g tapioca flour

3 tsp fresh thyme, chopped

1½ tsp cracked black pepper

1½ tsp gluten free baking powder

Sausages

6 vegetarian, dairy free, gluten free sausages

Preheat the oven to 200°C / Gas 6.

Brush the traybake tin with olive oil.

Place the vegetables, olive oil, salt, thyme, pepper and soy sauce in a roasting tin and gently mix together with a spatula. Roast for 20 minutes and set to one side.

Reduce the oven to 180°C / Gas 4.

Place all the batter ingredients into a large bowl and beat with an electric mixer on high speed for 1 minute or until well combined. Spread this mixture into the traybake tin. Partly submerge the sausages into the mixture then place the roasted vegetables on top and gently press them in so they are partly submerged as well. Bake for 20 minutes. You can tell the bake is done once the base is firm to the touch and golden in colour.

Best eaten warm from the oven

TIP

You can also crack eggs on top of this towards the end of the cooking time. They'll take 8-10 minutes to set

Open Avocado Sandwich on Almond Bread

MAKES 1 X 900G LOAF
FREE FROM GLUTEN / DAIRY

This bread is easy to make, neutral in flavour, and therefore very versatile. It can be baked, cooled, sliced and frozen. You can then quickly toast from frozen for a quick Scooby Snack.

Almond bread

350g ground almonds
165g ground golden flaxseed
2 tsp gluten free baking powder
½ tsp bicarbonate of soda
½ tsp salt
4 eggs
245ml coconut milk
125g dairy free coconut yoghurt

Avocado topping

2 ripe avocados
1 tsp cracked black pepper
½ fresh red chilli, finely chopped
Juice of ½ a lemon
½ tsp smoked, sweet paprika
2 tbsp dairy free coconut yoghurt
20g fresh coriander, chopped

Finishing

2 red peppers, sliced
180g sprouted seeds (we used Good4u Lentil Sprout Mix)
3 tbsp sweet chilli sauce, more if required

Preheat the oven to 170°C / Gas 3.

Line the loaf tin with baking parchment.

Place all the ingredients for the almond bread into a bowl and beat with an electric mixer on high speed for 1 minute. Add the mixture to the loaf tin. Bake for 45 minutes until springy to the touch; a flat cake skewer will come out clean when the loaf is ready. Leave the loaf to rest in its tin for 10 minutes before lifting out onto a wire rack to cool.

Increase the oven to 200°C / Gas 6.

Roast the sliced red peppers for 20-25 minutes until soft and the skin has slightly blackened. Allow to cool and set to one side.

Cut and toast however many slices of bread you require. Mash up the avocados with a fork, add the pepper, chilli, lemon juice, paprika, coconut yoghurt and coriander and mix well with a spatula.

Spread this mixture over the sliced, toasted bread and top with the roasted red pepper, sprouted seeds and drizzle with sweet chilli sauce.

The bread will keep in an airtight container for 3 days. Can be frozen

This bread pairs well with robust toppings. Try with Charlotte's Tomato Sauce (see page 194) or Olive Tapenade (see page 182)

SUNFLOWER

PUMPKIN

LINSEED

Oaty Coconut Bars

MAKES 1 TRAYBAKE
FREE FROM GLUTEN / DAIRY / NUTS

We've revisited the flapjack and had a go at lightening it up a little. Much as we adore butter, especially West Country butter, we have to admit this dairy free version is every bit as tasty.

115ml unrefined coconut oil, plus extra for brushing

100g Date Paste (see page 197)

2 eggs

1 tsp vanilla paste

185g gluten free rolled oats

85g dried cranberries

25g pumpkin seeds, toasted

25g sunflower seeds, toasted

25g golden linseeds, toasted

40g freeze-dried raspberries

Preheat the oven to 170°C / Gas 3.

Line the traybake tin with baking parchment and brush the paper with coconut oil.

Add the Date Paste to a bowl with the eggs, coconut oil and vanilla paste. Beat with an electric mixer on high speed for 1 minute. Then add the oats, cranberries and toasted seeds and stir in with a spatula. Finally, gently fold in the freeze-dried raspberries. Avoid over stirring otherwise the whole mixture will turn pink.

Spoon the mixture into the tin and spread evenly into the corners. You can leave the top quite rough and rustic looking.

Bake for 15-18 minutes until the mixture turns mid golden brown. It will feel firm to the touch. Leave in the tin to cool completely, then turn out and cut into slices.

Keeps in an airtight container for 5 days. Can be frozen

TIP

By using Date Paste, we've kept the sweetness quite subtle, therefore you may wish to add a tablespoon of liquid sweetener if you are of the sweet toothed tribe

MIXED SEEDS

DRIED CRANBERRIES

Sunbeam Muffins

MAKES 12 MUFFINS
FREE FROM GLUTEN / NUTS

The feta and honey work a wonderful sweet and salty magic in this recipe. As with all our muffin recipes, these are best eaten on the day, preferably still warm from the oven. Ideal for breakfast, or serve for lunch as part of a Ploughman's.

Muffins

85g polenta

75g milled flaxseed, sunflower and pumpkin seed blend

50g sorghum flour

2 tsp gluten free baking powder

½ tsp bicarbonate of soda

100ml rapeseed oil

100g runny honey

2 tbsp milk

2 eggs

100g Greek yoghurt

200g dried apricots, diced

140g vegetarian feta, crumbled

Topping

60g vegetarian feta, crumbled

85g runny honey

20g pine nuts, toasted

100g dried apricots, diced

Preheat the oven to 170°C / Gas 3.

Line a 12 hole muffin pan with paper muffin cases.

Place the polenta, milled seed, sorghum flour, baking powder and bicarbonate of soda into a bowl and combine with a fork.

Place the rapeseed oil, honey, milk, eggs and Greek yoghurt into another bowl and beat with an electric mixer on high speed for 1 minute until well combined.

Add the dry ingredients to the wet and mix with a fork until all the ingredients are combined. Then, with a spatula, lightly fold in the diced apricots and the 140g of crumbled feta.

Spoon the mixture into the muffin cases and top with the 60g of crumbled feta. Bake for 18-20 minutes until gently domed and springy to the touch. Leave for 2-3 minutes, and then carefully turn them out on to a rack.

Drizzle each muffin with the honey using a teaspoon and then sprinkle each muffin with toasted pine nuts and dried apricot. Allow to set. Eat slightly warm or leave to cool.

 *Omit the polenta, milled seed blend, sorghum flour, baking powder and bicarbonate of soda and replace with 200g gluten free self-raising flour.*

 Best eaten on the day. Can be frozen

 TIP For a more dramatic savoury vs. sweet effect, you can add snipped fresh thyme into the muffin batter

Roast Plum & Toasted Hazelnut Muffins

MAKES 12 MUFFINS
FREE FROM GLUTEN / DAIRY

I just can't leave these little scamps alone. Best eaten warm from the oven with a dollop of plum Half Jam (see page 197) on the side... beautifully simple.

Plum sauce

200g plums, pitted and diced

1 tbsp liquid sweetener of choice

A squeeze of lemon juice

½ tsp ground star anise

Topping

35g sunflower seeds

35g pumpkin seeds

20g hazelnuts, chopped and toasted

35g gluten free rolled oats

50g ground hazelnuts

3 tbsp liquid sweetener of choice, warmed

Muffins

35g hazelnuts, chopped and toasted

100ml rapeseed oil

100g liquid sweetener of choice

85g polenta

125g ground hazelnuts

1½ tsp gluten free baking powder

2 eggs

150g dairy free coconut yoghurt

Preheat the oven to 170°C / Gas 3.

Line a 12 hole muffin pan with paper muffin cases.

To make the plum sauce, place the diced plums in a pan on medium heat with the liquid sweetener, lemon juice and star anise. As the plums start to soften mash them with the back of a wooden spoon. Keep stirring the mixture for 3 minutes until you end up with a runny honey-like consistency. Set aside to cool.

Place all the topping ingredients into a bowl and mix with a spatula until well combined. Set to one side.

Place all the muffin ingredients into a bowl and beat with an electric mixer on high speed for approximately 1 minute until well combined. Then, gently fold the plum sauce into the mixture with a spatula so that you achieve a marbled effect.

Spoon the mixture into the muffin cases, filling to nearly the top. Divide the crumble topping evenly between the 12 muffins. Bake for 18-20 minutes until gently domed and springy to the touch. Leave for 2-3 minutes, then eat warm or carefully turn them out onto a rack and leave to cool completely.

Best eaten on the day. Can be frozen

TIP

To go nut free, swap the ground hazelnuts in the topping and muffin ingredients for a milled flaxseed, sunflower and pumpkin seed blend, and omit the chopped hazelnuts

2 tbsp Florentine Mix (see page 186)

Posh Porridge

FREE FROM GLUTEN / DAIRY / NUTS

A delicious, no dairy, no nut porridge full of goodness and packed to the rafters with flavour. Excellent midwinter fuel.

400ml coconut milk

SERVES 2

2 tbsp toasted coconut flakes

50g rolled gluten free porridge oats

20g quinoa flakes

Place the coconut milk, oats, quinoa flakes and honey in the microwave for 2 minutes on full power. Stir and then sprinkle the Florentine Mix and coconut flakes on top.

1½ tbsp runny honey

LOVELY

LUNCHES

Pasties, tarts, soup & quiche

Find somewhere comfy to relax and eat, a beautiful lunch on a beautiful seat

Asparagus & Watercress Frittata

MAKES 1 LARGE FRYING PAN'S WORTH
FREE FROM GLUTEN / NUTS

This is early summer captured in a frying pan. Effortless and super tasty. Serve as it is, or with some Triangle Toasties on the side (see page 31). Rather than a plate, we pop the whole frittata onto a rustic chopping board and let people help themselves.

Frittata

200g asparagus, trimmed and chopped

8 eggs

1 tsp ground white pepper

Finely grated zest of 1 lemon

60g vegetarian Italian hard cheese, grated, plus extra for topping

100g vegetarian cheddar, grated

½ tsp Lemon & Garlic Paste (see page 195)

85g watercress, washed and roughly chopped

1-2 tbsp olive oil

Bring a saucepan of water to the boil. Plunge the asparagus in and boil for exactly 1 minute, drain and rinse under cold water to stop it cooking any further.

Place the eggs, pepper, lemon zest, Italian hard cheese, cheddar and Lemon & Garlic Paste into a bowl and beat with an electric mixer on high speed for 1 minute. With a spatula, gently stir in the asparagus and the watercress to the egg mixture.

Preheat the olive oil in a non-stick frying pan. Pour the mixture into the pan and gently stir the frittata before it starts to set. Fry for 5-6 minutes on a medium to high heat. Whilst cooking, use a fish slice to loosen the frittata around the edges and underneath to make sure it is not sticking to the pan. Preheat the grill to maximum heat.

You'll end up with a partially set frittata with some liquid still in the centre. Sprinkle the extra Italian hard cheese over the top of the frittata before placing it, still in its pan, under the grill for 2-3 minutes or until lightly set. Slide from the pan to your serving plate.

Eat straight away.

Best eaten warm from the pan

If watercress is hard to come by, baby spinach leaves or rocket work well

OUR LOCAL CHEESE FESTIVAL IN
STURMINSTER NEWTON IS LOVELY
TO VISIT IF YOU ARE
EVER DOWN OUR WAY.
TWO MARQUEES FULL OF CHEESE,
CIDER AND MUSIC - IT DOESN'T
GET MUCH BETTER!
CHEESEFESTIVAL.CO.UK

Keeps in the fridge for
3 days. Can be frozen

TIP

Roasted red peppers and a little chopped fresh
chilli could be swapped for the butternut
squash if you want a bit of heat

Charlotte's Butternut Squash Quiche

MAKES 1 X 23CM LOOSE BOTTOMED FLAN TIN
FREE FROM GLUTEN / NUTS

This is a total winner. Everybody loves it and the brie works so well with the butternut squash. We're really lucky having so many artisan cheese makers on our doorstep.

Pastry

Butter, melted, for brushing

100g brown rice flour, plus extra for dusting

85g butter, diced

50g cornflour

50g ground golden flaxseed

½ tsp dried red chilli flakes

½ tsp black onion seeds

1 sprig fresh rosemary

½ tsp cracked black pepper

1 egg

2 tsp milk

Filling

Approximately ⅓ butternut squash, 300g raw weight, peeled and chopped into 3cm cubes

1 tbsp olive oil

½ tsp salt

½ tsp cracked black pepper

1 tsp butter

2 garlic cloves, crushed

100g spinach leaves, washed and dried

2 eggs

2 tbsp crème fraiche

60-100ml milk

125g vegetarian cheddar, grated

150g vegetarian brie, cut into fairly thin slices

1½ tbsp pine nuts, toasted

Preheat the oven to 180°C / Gas 4.

Brush the flan tin with melted butter.

Place all of the pastry ingredients, except the egg and milk, in a food processor and blitz until the mixture has the consistency of breadcrumbs. Add the egg and milk and blitz again for 30 seconds to 1 minute until a soft dough is formed.

The pastry is quite delicate, so is best pressed into the tin rather than rolled. Dust your hands and work surface liberally with rice flour, knead the dough briefly, and then form it into a ball. Put it into the tin and press firmly over the base and up the sides, making sure you have no holes. Don't worry about the pastry being a little bit bumpy. The tin can be lined with the pastry the day before, then covered and chilled overnight if you like to prep ahead.

Place the butternut squash in a roasting tin, drizzle with olive oil and sprinkle with the salt and pepper. Roast for 25 minutes or until soft.

Place a frying pan on a medium heat and add the butter and garlic for 2 minutes before adding the spinach. Cook for a further 1 minute until the spinach begins to wilt, then set to one side to cool.

Put the eggs and crème fraiche into a measuring jug and make up the liquid to 300ml with milk. Whisk until the eggs are well beaten and the mixture is bubbly.

Scatter the grated cheddar over the pastry and place the roasted butternut squash on top. Evenly layer the cooked spinach on top and then cover with the slices of brie. Carefully pour the egg mixture over the filling, stopping approximately ½cm from the top of the pastry. Sprinkle with the toasted pine nuts.

Bake for 35-40 minutes, until the top is set and golden brown but still slightly wobbly. The melted brie will look quite runny but it's important to make sure the egg mixture is set.

Serve hot or cold. If serving hot, leave in the tin for 5 minutes to settle before sliding onto a serving plate. If serving cold simply leave in the tin until required.

Curried Cauliflower Tart

MAKES 1 X 23CM LOOSE BOTTOMED FLAN TIN
FREE FROM GLUTEN / DAIRY / NUTS

It's true, you will need to set aside a bit of time to build this tart of several layers...but we reckon it's well worth the effort. Whilst developing this recipe we had to guard our results from the Honeybuns team, who would wander casually into the kitchen, tracing the aroma to its source. As with all things curried, this tart develops in flavour over a couple of days. Serve with the stupendously good apple pickle made by Linda Browne at burgessandbrowne.com

Pastry

Rapeseed oil, for brushing

100g brown rice flour, plus extra for dusting

50g cornflour

50g ground golden flaxseed

85g rapeseed oil

2 tsp black onion seeds

½ tsp turmeric

1 tsp gluten free madras curry powder

2 eggs

2 tsp coconut milk

Curry topping

1 tsp mustard seeds

1 tsp coriander seeds

1 tsp cumin seeds

2 tbsp rapeseed oil

1 onion, chopped

2 garlic cloves, chopped

2 tbsp gluten free madras curry powder

1 small cauliflower, trimmed and chopped

100g dried red lentils

½ lemon

200ml coconut milk

1 tsp black onion seeds, for sprinkling

Filling

Rapeseed oil

1 tsp cumin seeds

¼ tsp salt

¼ tsp cracked black pepper

100g spinach leaves, washed and dried

125g dairy free coconut yoghurt

4–5 tbsp of gluten free mango chutney

½ tsp ground coriander

1 egg, lightly beaten

Preheat the oven to 170°C / Gas 3.

Brush the flan tin with rapeseed oil. Dust a work surface with brown rice flour.

To make the pastry, place all the ingredients except the eggs and coconut milk, in a food processor and blitz until the mixture is the consistency of fine breadcrumbs. Add the eggs and coconut milk and blend until a soft dough is formed. Tip the dough onto the floured work surface and lightly knead. The mixture is a little crumbly to begin with, but it will come together after kneading. Flour your work surface again and roll out the dough to fit the bottom and sides of your tin. Roll the pastry gently around your rolling pin, and then unroll it over your flan tin. Press into the bottom and sides of the tin. Don't worry if the pastry breaks a little, you can just patch it up with some of the trimmings. Roll the rolling pin over the top edge of the tin to trim off any surplus pastry. You can use these bits to patch up any holes or cracks you have. Place the pastry lined tin in the fridge.

For the curry topping, roughly crush the mustard, coriander and cumin seeds in a pestle and mortar. Add the rapeseed oil to a non-stick frying pan and place on a medium heat. Add the onion, garlic, crushed seeds and curry powder to the pan. Fry for 5 minutes or until the onion starts to soften, then add the cauliflower, lentils, lemon and coconut milk. Turn the heat to low and simmer for 20 minutes. Stir occasionally to make sure the bottom of the mixture is not burning. Once cooked, set aside to cool and discard the lemon.

For the filling, heat a frying pan on a medium heat with the rapeseed oil, cumin seeds, salt and pepper and cook for 2 minutes before adding the spinach. Cook for a further 1-2 minutes until the leaves are just starting to wilt. Remove from the pan and place in a bowl, spreading out well to cool. Place the coconut yoghurt, mango chutney, ground coriander and egg in another bowl and beat for 1 minute with an electric mixer on high speed until the ingredients are combined.

To assemble the tart, place the spinach in the bottom of your unbaked pastry case, then add the coconut yoghurt mixture, then the curry and finish with a sprinkling of black onion seeds.

Bake for 30-35 minutes until the filling is set, turning golden in colour and the pastry is golden and crispy on the edges. Serve warm.

Keeps in the fridge for 3 days

TIP
The cauliflower can be swapped for any firmish vegetable such as potato or parsnip. Avoid any vegetables with a high water content like aubergines, lest they turn to mush

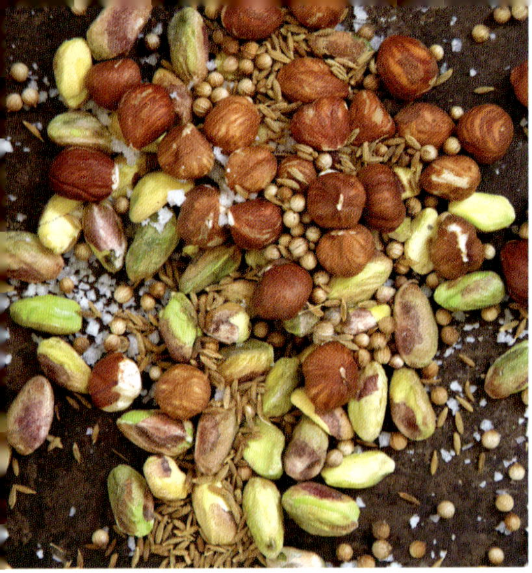
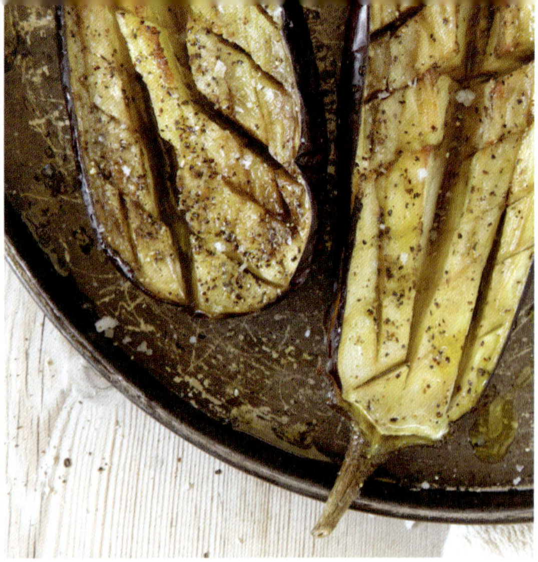
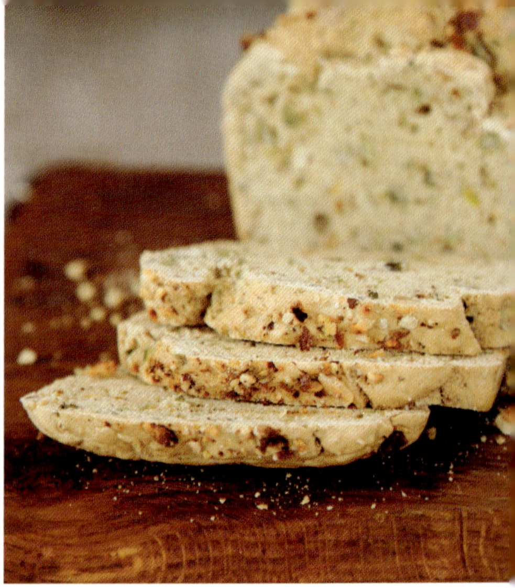
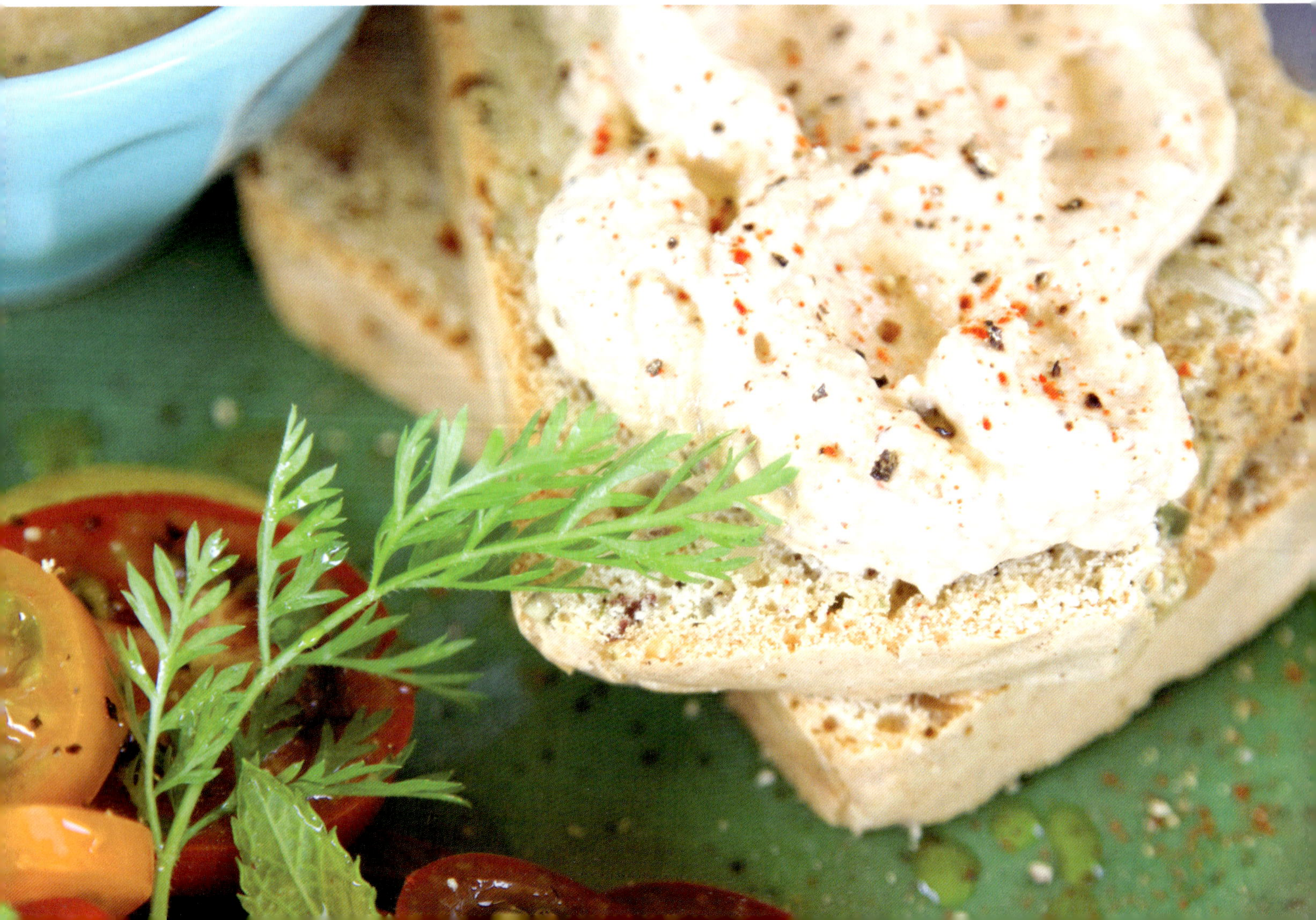

Seeded Loaf with Aubergine Spread

MAKES 1 X 900G LOAF
FREE FROM GLUTEN / DAIRY / NUTS

This is a beautifully soft bread, packed to the rafters with seeds. It slices well and can be used for sandwiches or toast. We've kept the flavour neutral, so you can pair it with robust, full on toppings. You can add herbs, spices or roasted vegetables to the dough if you want to ratchet up the flavour.

Multi seeded loaf

Rapeseed oil, for brushing

165g tapioca flour

350g milled flaxseed, sunflower and pumpkin seed blend

2 tsp gluten free baking powder

½ tsp bicarbonate of soda

½ tsp salt

100g sunflower seeds, toasted

8 egg whites

245ml coconut milk

125ml rapeseed oil

Aubergine spread

1 aubergine

Rapeseed oil, for brushing

1 garlic clove, crushed

¼ tsp sweet smoked paprika

¼ tsp salt

¼ tsp cracked black pepper

Juice of ½ a lemon

2 tsp tahini

2 tbsp dairy free cream cheese

12 oregano leaves, chopped

Preheat the oven to 170°C / Gas 3.

Line the loaf tin with baking parchment and brush the paper with rapeseed oil.

Add the tapioca flour, milled seed blend, baking powder, bicarbonate of soda, salt and toasted sunflower seeds to a mixing bowl. In another bowl whisk the egg whites, coconut milk and rapeseed oil until well combined.

Add the wet to the dry ingredients, and beat with an electric mixer on high speed for 1 minute. Pour into the loaf tin and bake for 40 minutes. The loaf will rise rather spectacularly and will crack along the top. The top will be crusty and firm and a cake skewer should come out cleanly when the loaf is ready. Leave the loaf in the tin for 10-15 minutes before turning out onto a wire rack to cool completely.

Increase the oven to 190°C / Gas 5.

Prick the aubergine all over with a fork, brush with a little rapeseed oil and place in a roasting tray. Roast in the oven for 30-35 minutes until the aubergine has collapsed and is very soft in the middle. Set aside to cool.

Slice the aubergine in half lengthways, and with a spoon scoop out the pulp leaving the skin behind. Place the pulp in a food processor along with the other aubergine spread ingredients and blitz until a spreadable paste is formed. It will still retain some texture.

Once the loaf has completely cooled, slice and spread thickly with the aubergine paste.

The loaf will keep for 3 days wrapped in clingfilm (it can also be frozen). The dip will keep for 3 days in the fridge

For the loaf: if you want a nice bit of warmth, try adding a couple of tablespoons of the Dukkah Spice (see page 185)

TRY A SCOOP OF
SUPER SOUP

Pea, Nettle & Mint Soup with Lemony Croutons

SOUP SERVES 4
FREE FROM GLUTEN / NUTS

With the addition of springtime nettle tips this pea soup gains a cheeky little kick, not dissimilar to adding fresh chilli. Swirled with crème fraiche and enjoyed with our flavoursome croutons it will easily keep you going 'til suppertime. You need the young May time nettle tips or use chopped fresh chilli if you prefer.

Soup

550ml gluten free vegetable stock
(we use Kallo vegetable organic stock cubes)

400g frozen or fresh peas

2 generous sprigs of fresh mint

¼ tsp salt

½ tsp cracked black pepper

2 tsp Lemon & Garlic Paste (see page 195)

Handful of young nettle tips or ½ fresh chilli, chopped

Finishing

Half a batch of Lemony Croutons (see page 188)

Bring the stock to the boil in a saucepan, turn down to a simmer and add the rest of the soup ingredients. Simmer for 3-5 minutes, or until the peas are just cooked. Remove from the heat and blitz in a food processor until smooth. Transfer the soup from the food processor back into the saucepan and return to a medium heat until warmed through.

Serve the soup warm with the croutons.

Soup and croutons can be frozen

TIP
Serve with a dollop of crème fraiche with a little lemon zest stirred in for extra va va voom

Naish Farm Muffins

MAKES 12 MUFFINS
FREE FROM GLUTEN / NUTS

These are perfect for picnics and packed lunches. They also work really well served with a ploughman's instead of bread. As with all muffins, these are best eaten on the day or you can freeze them once cooled on the day of baking.

Muffins

100ml rapeseed oil

2 eggs

50g sorghum flour

25g milled flaxseed, sunflower and pumpkin seed blend

50g tapioca flour

85g polenta

1 tsp sweet smoked paprika

100g vegetarian ricotta cheese

3 tbsp gluten free and vegetarian beer

75g fresh vegetarian Italian hard cheese, grated

2 tsp gluten free wholegrain mustard

1½ tsp gluten free baking powder

½ tsp bicarbonate of soda

Finishing

½ tsp per muffin (6 tsp overall) of a good quality, gluten free tomato chutney

50g vegetarian cheddar or fresh vegetarian Italian hard cheese, grated

Preheat the oven to 200°C / Gas 6.

Line a 12 hole muffin pan with paper muffin cases.

Place all the muffin ingredients into a mixing bowl. Mix well with an electric mixer on high speed for 1 minute until well combined.

Place a small spoonful of the mixture into each muffin case and make a hollow with the back of a spoon. Into the hollow space you have made place ½ teaspoon of chutney. Next, distribute the rest of the mixture over the chutney to conceal it. Sprinkle the top of each muffin with the cheddar or Italian hard cheese.

Bake in the oven for 12 minutes.

Leave for 2-3 minutes, before carefully turning them out onto a rack to cool.

Omit the sorghum flour, milled seed blend, tapioca flour and polenta and replace with 210g gluten free self-raising flour. Instead of 1½ teaspoon baking powder, just use ½ teaspoon.

Best eaten on the day. Can be frozen

TIP

Cider works really well instead of the ale and is naturally gluten free to boot. For the chutney we highly recommend The Dorset Blue Cheese Company's 'Spiced Tomato Chutney'

Saag Aloo Tart

MAKES 1 X 23CM LOOSE BOTTOMED FLAN TIN
FREE FROM GLUTEN / DAIRY / NUTS

*If you like the flavours of this classic Indian side dish, then
this tart's got your name on it. True, it will take a little time to
collate the ingredients, but it's more than worth the effort. In
order to simplify things a little, pre-mix the spices so you can
add them all at once, rather than measuring them out singly.*

Pastry

Rapeseed oil, for brushing

100g brown rice flour, plus
extra for dusting

50g cornflour

50g ground golden flaxseed

85g vegetarian margarine

2 tsp black onion seeds

½ tsp turmeric

1 tsp gluten free Madras
curry powder

½ tsp cracked black pepper

1 egg

2 tsp plant-based milk

Yoghurt layer

125g dairy free
coconut yoghurt

4-5 tbsp of gluten free
mango chutney

½ tsp ground coriander

1 tsp cumin seeds

¼ tsp salt

¼ tsp cracked black pepper

1 egg

Filling

750g washed new potatoes,
boiled until cooked

3 tbsp rapeseed oil

2 tsp cumin seeds

2 tsp coriander seeds

1 tsp turmeric

1 tsp black onion seeds

1 tsp fennel seeds

2 tsp mustard seeds

¼ tsp ground cardamom

1 tsp ground ginger

½ tsp chilli flakes

3 garlic cloves, chopped

1 onion, sliced

100g spinach leaves, washed
and dried

Preheat the oven to 170°C / Gas 3.

Brush the flan tin with rapeseed oil. Dust a work surface
with brown rice flour.

To make the pastry, place all the ingredients, except the
egg and milk, into a food processor and blitz until the
mixture is the consistency of fine breadcrumbs. Add the
egg and milk and blend until a soft dough is formed. Tip
the dough onto the floured work surface and lightly knead.
The mixture is a little crumbly to begin with, but it will come
together after kneading.

Flour your work surface again and roll out the dough to
fit the bottom and sides of your tin. Roll the pastry gently
around your rolling pin, and then unroll it over your flan tin.
Press into the bottom and sides of the tin. Don't worry if
the pastry breaks a little, you can just patch it up with some
of the trimmings. Roll the rolling pin over the top edge of
the tin to trim off any surplus pastry. You can use these bits
to patch up any holes or cracks you have. Place the pastry
lined tin in the fridge.

To make the filling, chop the new potatoes into 1cm cubes
and set aside. Add the rapeseed oil to a non-stick frying
pan and place on a medium heat. Add all the spices and
chopped garlic to this pan and stir constantly to prevent
burning. You may find the seeds pop a little, if so turn your
heat down a bit. Crush any whole seeds in the pan using the
back of a wooden spoon.

Next, add the onion slices to the pan and cook until they
start to soften. Add the chopped potatoes, and turn them
around in the spiced oil to ensure they take on all the
colours and flavours. You do not need to stir too much
as you are looking to impart some fried golden colour
onto the potatoes. When the potatoes have mostly turned
yellow, place the spinach on top. Within a minute or so the
spinach will start to wilt. At this point stir the spinach into
the potatoes. Set to one side to cool.

To make the yoghurt layer, place all the ingredients in a
bowl and beat with an electric mixer on high speed for 1
minute until the ingredients are combined.

To assemble the tart, place the yoghurt layer into the
bottom of the tart, then add the potato and spinach
mixture, packing them in quite tightly so that you cannot
see the yoghurt layer in the bottom.

Bake for 30-35 minutes until the filling it set, turning golden
in colour and the pastry is golden and crispy on the edges.
Serve warm or cold.

Keeps in the fridge in an
airtight container for 3 days

TIP

The pastry case can be made
ahead of time and frozen

Mmmm... mushroomy

Keeps in the fridge for 3 days

TIP

You could make a pie instead of a pasty by popping the filling in a pie dish and hand crimping the pastry lid on top

Giant Mushroom Pasty

MAKES 1 LARGE PASTY, SERVES 4-6
FREE FROM GLUTEN / NUTS

This looks a little bit like a giant Cornish Pasty. As the pastry is quite short it is prone to breaking up a little more than pastry containing gluten. You will need to handle it with a little care when forming the "pasty" shape.

Mushroom filling

1-2 tbsp cornflour

250g chestnut mushrooms, sliced

250g of button mushrooms, halved

3 cloves of garlic, crushed

1 white onion, finely diced

1 tbsp olive oil

1½ tsp paprika

1 tsp butter

½ tsp chilli flakes

½ tsp fresh or dried oregano

½ tsp fresh or dried rosemary

½ tsp cumin seeds

¼ tsp cracked black pepper

2 tbsp crème fraiche

1 tbsp double cream

Pastry

100g brown rice flour, plus extra for dusting

85g butter, diced

50g cornflour

50g ground golden flaxseed

½ tsp cumin seeds

½ tsp black onion seeds

¼ tsp salt

¼ tsp cracked black pepper

2 eggs

2 tsp milk

Finishing

1 egg yolk mixed with a dash of milk, for brushing

¼ tsp cumin seeds, for sprinkling

¼ tsp black onion seeds, for sprinkling

Preheat the oven to 200°C / Gas 6.

Starting with the mushroom filling, in a small bowl mix the cornflour with a little cold water, using just enough to make a paste. Set to one side.

Cook all the filling ingredients, except the crème fraiche and double cream, in a deep sided frying pan on a medium to high heat until cooked through and the mushrooms have browned off. This will take around 5-6 minutes. Add the crème fraiche and double cream, and boil fiercely for 1-2 minutes until the cream thickens, stirring regularly to avoid sticking to the pan. To thicken the filling, remove the pan from the heat before adding the pre-mixed cornflour paste, a tablespoon at a time (you're aiming for the consistency of thick yoghurt). Whisk vigorously with a hand whisk until the cornflour has fully dissolved. Set the pan aside to cool down.

Mix all the pastry ingredients, except the eggs and milk, in a food processor until the mixture has the consistency of breadcrumbs. Add the eggs and milk and blend until a soft dough is formed.

Dust your hands liberally with brown rice flour and place the pastry between 2 sheets of baking parchment (cut to the size of the baking sheet). Take care to position it centrally as the bottom sheet will be used to bake the pasty. Using a rolling pin, roll out the pastry into a 25cm circle and about ½cm thick.

Peel the top sheet of baking parchment off the pastry and spoon the mushroom filling onto one half of the pastry leaving approximately 2cm edge. Brush the edges of the pastry with the beaten egg yolk and fold the pastry over using the baking parchment that the pasty is sat on, so that it forms a large pasty shape.

Crimp the edges together by pressing down with your thumb, forming a seal around the edge. Brush the top of the pasty with the beaten egg yolk and milk mix and sprinkle with cumin seeds and black onion seeds. Transfer the pasty and bottom sheet of baking parchment onto the baking sheet.

Bake for 30-35 minutes or until golden brown.

Artichoke & Falafel Bake

**MAKES 1 X 20CM X 7CM DEEP
ROUND OVEN DISH
FREE FROM GLUTEN / DAIRY / NUTS**

This is one of our favourite standby lunches for any VIP visitors to the bakery we need to impress. You can make the falafels up in advance and freeze them. Serve with a simple leaf salad and a selection of tapenades on the side (see page 182). You can buy marinated artichokes from delis and most supermarkets.

Falafels

400g tinned chickpeas, drained

1 large onion, chopped

2 cloves garlic, chopped

2 tbsp chickpea flour

1 tbsp fresh parsley

3 tsp Dukkah Spice (see page 185)

½ tsp salt

½ tsp cracked black pepper

Base

150g marinated artichoke hearts, roughly chopped

Olive oil, for drizzling

3 tsp Dukkah Spice (see page 185)

Batter

3 eggs

2 tbsp quinoa flour

2 tbsp chickpea flour

3 tbsp coconut milk

1 tbsp rapeseed oil

3 tsp Dukkah Spice (see page 185)

1 tsp turmeric

Topping

2 tsp fennel seeds, toasted

Preheat the oven to 180°C / Gas 4.

Line a baking sheet with baking parchment.

For the falafels, place all the ingredients in a food processor and blitz for 1 minute until a textured paste is formed. Divide evenly into 12 balls and hand roll until compact. Pop the falafels onto the baking sheet and into the oven for 15 minutes.

For the base, pop the chopped artichoke into the oven dish and drizzle with olive oil and sprinkle with the Dukkah Spice. Bake for 5 minutes before setting to one side.

Place the batter ingredients into a bowl and beat with an electric mixer on high speed until smooth. This will take 1-2 minutes.

Place the falafels on top of the artichokes in the oven dish and then pour the batter in and around the falafels. Sprinkle with the toasted fennel seeds. Bake for 15-20 minutes, or until golden brown and firm. Serve warm.

Best eaten on the day, served warm

TIP

Try adding a little fresh chopped chilli and a handful of chopped Oven Roasted Tomatoes (see page 195) to the batter

Very Green Summer Tart

MAKES 1 X 23CM LOOSE BOTTOMED FLAN TIN
FREE FROM GLUTEN / NUTS

Packed to bursting with vibrant fresh green veg and herbs, this looks beautiful served with pea shoots and shavings of vegetarian Italian hard cheese. We've included our favourite vegetables, but you can adapt to include seasonal goodies.

Pastry

Melted butter, for brushing

100g brown rice flour

25g spinach leaves, washed and dried

85g butter, diced and chilled

50g cornflour, plus extra for dusting

50g ground golden flaxseed

1 tsp black onion seeds

½ tsp fresh rosemary, chopped

¼ tsp salt

¼ tsp cracked black pepper

1 egg

2 tsp milk

Filling

150g new potatoes, peeled

2 tbsp of Lemon & Garlic Paste (see page 195)

12 spears of fresh asparagus, trimmed

1 small courgette, cut into ½cm slices

Rapeseed oil, for brushing

125g vegetarian cheddar, grated

50g peas, fresh or frozen and thawed

1 tbsp Peasto (see page 181) or vegetarian pesto

Handful of fresh mint, chopped

50g vegetarian feta cheese, crumbled coarsely

100ml milk

2 heaped tbsp sour cream

2 eggs

30g pumpkin seeds

Preheat the oven to 170°C / Gas 3.

Brush the flan tin with melted butter, and place a disc of baking parchment in the bottom.

To make the pastry, place all the ingredients, except the egg and milk, into a food processor and blitz for 1 minute until the mixture has the consistency of breadcrumbs. Add the egg and milk and blitz until a soft dough is formed. Dust your hands and a rolling pin with cornflour. Turn the dough out onto a clean worktop sprinkled liberally with cornflour and roll out to fit the bottom and sides of your tin, trimming off any excess pastry from around the top of the tin.

Bring a lidded pan of lightly salted water to the boil and add the potatoes. Boil until a knife can slide through the potatoes with ease, approximately 15 minutes depending on size. You do not want them too soft or they will become a pulp. When ready, drain them and whilst still warm cut into 1cm thick slices. Place the sliced potatoes in a bowl, spoon the Lemon & Garlic Paste over the top and set to one side.

Bring a pan of lightly salted water to the boil, pop the asparagus in and bring back to the boil for 3 minutes. Drain the asparagus and retain the hot water in another pan. Re-use this water to boil the courgette for 2 minutes and then drain. Spread the asparagus and courgette out on a plate to cool.

Brush your griddle pan with rapeseed oil and place on a high heat. Place the asparagus spears in the hot pan and press them down using a wooden spoon so that you get the lovely lines from the pan onto the asparagus. Repeat the process with the rest of the vegetables. Keep brushing the griddle pan with rapeseed oil between vegetables.

Into your prepared pastry case place the cheddar, grilled vegetables and peas (you may need to cut the asparagus spears down to fit). With a teaspoon, place little dollops of the Peasto all over the top of the flan. Sprinkle with the mint and feta cheese.

Place the milk, sour cream and eggs into a bowl and beat with an electric mixer on high speed for 1 minute until the ingredients have combined. Slowly pour this mixture all over the flan, allowing for the creamy mixture to soak down in amongst the vegetables. Sprinkle with the pumpkin seeds.

Bake in the oven for 35-40 minutes until the filling in the middle has set and is mid golden in colour.

Keeps in the fridge for 3 days. Can be frozen

TIP

The veggies for the filling can be prepared the day before. The pastry can also be made ahead and you can line your tin and store in the fridge

Courgette, Blue Vinny & Roasted Garlic Traybake

MAKES 1 TRAYBAKE
FREE FROM GLUTEN / NUTS

We served this straight from the oven on our "Big Dig" tree planting day at Honeybuns (see Em's blog). Served with a hearty soup on a wintry day, this is an absolute corker. Freezes really well too. Dorset Blue Vinny is made just a mile down the lane from us. Find them at dorsetblue.com

Traybake

100g polenta

55g tapioca flour

55g sorghum flour

1 tsp cracked black pepper

2 tsp gluten free baking powder

3 eggs

100ml milk

1 courgette, trimmed and grated

100g Dorset Blue Vinny, crumbled

1 tbsp Lemon & Garlic Paste (see page 195), or use shop bought garlic and ginger paste

200g butter, melted

Topping

40g vegetarian Italian hard cheese, grated

A few pine nuts to sprinkle over the top (optional)

Preheat the oven to 180°C / Gas 4.

Line the traybake tin with baking parchment.

Place the polenta, tapioca flour, sorghum flour, pepper and baking powder into a mixing bowl and sift with a fork.

In another bowl, place the eggs, milk, grated courgette, Blue Vinny, Lemon & Garlic Paste together with the melted butter. Beat with an electric mixer on high speed for approximately 1 minute until well combined. Add this mixture to the bowl of dry ingredients and beat again for approximately 1 minute until a batter is formed.

Spoon the mixture into the tin and then sprinkle the Italian hard cheese over the top, and pine nuts, if using.

Bake for 18-20 minutes until mid golden brown in colour and springy to the touch.

 *Omit the polenta, tapioca and sorghum flour and replace with 210g of gluten free self-raising flour and reduce the baking powder to 1 teaspoon.*

 Best eaten warm from the tin. Keeps in the fridge for 3 days. Can be frozen

 TIP Vegetarian Italian hard cheese works well too in the traybake if you fancy a change from Blue Vinny

say cheese

Keeps in the fridge for
1 day. Can be frozen

TIP

You can bake the base ahead
of time, cut into portions and freeze.
Then toast from frozen

Posh Rarebit

MAKES 1 X 450G LOAF
SERVES 4
FREE FROM GLUTEN / NUTS

This is our take on cheese and tomato on toast. Instead of toast, we've created a superbly versatile base, which can be topped with anything tasty you have in the larder or growing in the garden.

Roasted red onion and red pepper

1 red onion, chopped into roughly 1cm chunks

1 red pepper, chopped into 1cm chunks

1 tbsp olive oil, plus extra for brushing

¼ tsp salt

¼ tsp cracked black pepper

Roasted tomatoes

2 salad tomatoes, sliced into roughly 2cm chunks

Olive oil, for brushing and drizzling

Gluten free balsamic vinegar, for drizzling

½ tsp cracked black pepper

Base

3 eggs

100g quinoa flakes

25g polenta

4 tbsp olive oil

1 tbsp onion marmalade

1 tsp gluten free baking powder

½ tsp black onion seeds

½ tsp cumin seeds

Topping

1 tbsp olive oil

1 large red onion, cut into roughly 2cm chunks

3 tsp quinoa flour

1 tsp gluten free Worcestershire sauce

¼ tsp Tabasco sauce

4 tbsp gluten free tomato chutney
(to spread on the cooked base)

200g vegetarian mature cheddar, grated

1 tsp dried oregano, for sprinkling

Preheat the oven to 180°C / Gas 4.

Brush 2 roasting tins with olive oil. Line the loaf tin with baking parchment and brush the paper with olive oil.

In one of the roasting tins, place the onion, red pepper, olive oil, salt and pepper, and mix together with your hands or a spoon to ensure all the ingredients are combined. In the other roasting tin, place the tomatoes, drizzle with olive oil and balsamic vinegar, then sprinkle with the pepper. Roast both tins for 15 minutes and then set aside to cool

Place the base ingredients into a bowl and beat with an electric mixer on high speed for 1 minute until the ingredients are combined and you have a smooth mixture. Stir in the slightly cooled roasted onion and pepper with a wooden spoon. Spoon the mixture into the loaf tin and bake for 20-25 minutes or until golden brown and firm to the touch.

Allow the bread to cool completely, then slice lengthways as if opening up a baguette. Then cut the 2 halves in half again widthways so you end up with 4 quarters. Toast these pieces either by putting them in a toaster, or placing the pieces on a baking sheet and putting them under the grill until they are golden brown. Cover them with foil to keep warm.

Warm the olive oil in a frying pan on a medium heat, add the red onion, turn the heat down and stir until just starting to soften. This will take 4-5 minutes. Still on the low heat, add the quinoa flour, Worcestershire and Tabasco sauce, and stir until combined. Finally add the roasted tomatoes and gently stir these in so as not to mush them up.

Spread the tomato chutney on top of each quarter, and then quickly spoon the red onion mixture over the toast and chutney. Sprinkle the cheddar and dried oregano over the top and pop into the oven for 10-12 minutes or until golden brown all over and with a slight crust on the cheese.

Delicious served warm from the oven with a crisp green salad, juicy tomatoes from the greenhouse and a balsamic salad dressing.

TEATIME

TREATS

Tarts, cakes, buns & bakes

If you fancy something deliciously sweet, then put on your pinny and cook up a treat

♡ HOME MADE ♡

Blackcurrant & Elderflower Cakelets

MAKES 12 CAKELETS
FREE FROM GLUTEN / NUTS

Neither a cup cake nor a muffin; these little flat top cakelets are delectably different. Perfect for a summer tea break in the garden.

Cakelets

70g butter

2 tbsp blackcurrant jam

115g crystallised sweetener of choice

100g sorghum flour

50g shelled hemp

1 tsp gluten free baking powder

2 eggs

70g crème fraiche

½ tsp vanilla paste

½ tbsp elderflower cordial

140g fresh or frozen blackcurrants

Drench

2 tbsp elderflower cordial

Juice of 1 lemon

Topping

Icing sugar (we use golden), for dusting

3 fresh blackcurrants per cakelet

Fresh elderflowers, for sprinkling

Preheat the oven to 170°C / Gas 3.

Line a 12 hole muffin pan with paper muffin cases.

Melt the butter and allow it to cool slightly before adding to a bowl with all of the cakelet ingredients, except the blackcurrants. Beat with an electric mixer on high speed for 1 minute until smooth and well combined. Then gently fold in the blackcurrants using a spatula.

Spoon this mixture evenly between the cases, filling them three quarters full to avoid the cakes spilling over.

Bake for 18-20 minutes until they are springy to the touch.

To make the drench, mix the cordial and lemon juice in a little jug. Whilst still hot from the oven, prick each cakelet deeply with a cake skewer or cocktail stick several times. Pour a share of the drench over each cakelet.

Pop the cakelets on a rack to cool completely.

For the topping, dust each cakelet with sieved icing sugar and arrange fruit and flowers on top, as you wish.

Best eaten on the day. Can be frozen

TIP

You can use frozen fruit if fresh is hard to come by, just defrost them before using or they will freeze your mixture solid

juicy

lovely

oranges

St Clements Cake

MAKES 1 TRAYBAKE
FREE FROM GLUTEN / NUTS

If you can resist eating this beauty for a couple of days, a lovely marmalade flavour develops as the citrus oils mingle and infuse the whole cake.

Cake

3 eggs

100g sorghum flour

140g milled flaxseed, sunflower and pumpkin seed blend

2½ tsp gluten free baking powder

225g crystallised sweetener of choice

2 tbsp lemon curd

1 tsp orange oil

Grated zest of 2 oranges

Grated zest of 1 lemon

Juice of 2 oranges and 1 lemon, to make 50ml

300g butter, melted

Topping

2 oranges

3 tbsp marmalade

Preheat the oven to 170°C / Gas 3.

Line the traybake tin with baking parchment.

Crack the eggs into a mixing bowl and add the other cake ingredients. Beat with an electric mixer on high speed for 1 minute until smooth and well combined. Spoon and spread the mixture evenly into the tin.

Slice the oranges as thinly as possible. You can do this by hand or use a mandoline slicer. To prevent the orange slices from sinking too much, place them on top of the cake halfway through the bake time.

Bake for 25 minutes, until springy to the touch.

Leave the cake in the tin to cool completely, then turn out onto a rack.

Heat the marmalade in the microwave for 30 seconds on full power or until it is runny. With a pastry brush gently glaze the orange slices.

TIP

Keep in an airtight container for 3 days. Can be frozen

For extra decadence, sandwich slices together with lemon curd or marmalade. Pink grapefruit slices would look lovely as an alternative topping

Chai, Date & Apple Pud-cake

MAKES 1 TRAYBAKE
FREE FROM GLUTEN / DAIRY

Each year we take our lovely pop up Honeybuns café to Glastonbury Festival. One of our off-duty treats is to head up to the Greenfields to sip chai tea. This got me thinking about creating a versatile chai cake come pudding and so, here it is. Gorgeous served warm with dairy free ice cream.

Cake

325g rapeseed oil

225g demerara sugar, light or dark

200g ground almonds

185g sorghum flour

3 tsp gluten free baking powder

4 eggs

1 large cooking apple, cored, peeled and grated

¼ tsp vanilla paste

1-1½ tsp Chai Spice (see page 185)

350g dates, chopped

Topping

2 large cooking apples, cored, peeled and sliced

Demerara sugar (light or dark), for sprinkling

Preheat the oven to 170°C / Gas 3.

Line the traybake tin with baking parchment.

Pop all the cake ingredients into a bowl and mix with an electric mixer on high speed for 1 minute until well combined. Spoon the cake mixture into the tin, cover with the sliced apple, sprinkle with demerara sugar and bake for 40-45 minutes. The cake is ready when springy to the touch and a flat cake skewer will come out moist but clean.

Leave in the tin for 10 minutes before lifting out onto a rack to cool.

Keeps in the fridge for 3 days. Can be frozen

TIP

If time is short to make the Chai Spice mix, use Drink Me Chai spiced chai latte blend instead noting that this contains dairy. Find them at drinkmechai.co.uk

Moreish Shortbreads

**MAKES 25 LITTLE STAR SHAPED BISCUITS
FREE FROM GLUTEN**

*Growing up with three ever ravenous brothers, it was a
big deal getting to the cake tin in our house before these
had all been snaffled. Try sandwiching them together with
Chocolate Banana Spread (see page 196) and half dipping
in dark chocolate for extra va va voom.*

25g almonds, chopped and toasted

85g butter, chilled and cubed

85g ground almonds

70g polenta, plus extra for dusting

60g demerara sugar

½ tsp ground star anise

Preheat the oven to 170°C / Gas 3.

Line a baking sheet with baking parchment.

Place all the ingredients in a food processor and blitz for
1-2 minutes until a soft dough has formed, or rub the
butter into the dry ingredients using your fingertips until a
soft pliable dough is formed. Doing it by hand will take 3-4
minutes. It'll be a lovely rich caramel colour when ready.
Wrap the dough in clingfilm and chill for 30 minutes before
rolling out.

Liberally dust a work surface and rolling pin with polenta.
Roll your dough out to approximately 1cm thickness and cut
out your biscuits. We used a star shaped cutter, 5cm across.

Space out your biscuits on the baking sheet, and bake for
8-10 minutes. They turn a deep golden colour when ready.

Once out of the oven, allow to rest for 5 minutes before
transferring them using a fish slice to a rack to cool.

Keeps in an airtight
container for 7 days.
Can be frozen

TIP

You can morph these cookies into Easter
or Christmas treats by half dipping them
in melted chocolate and sprinkling with
crystallised chopped fruits or zests

Chocolate, Orange & Cardamom Biscotti

MAKES 16-18 BISCOTTI
FREE FROM GLUTEN / DAIRY / NUTS

These are nothing like their dry, pre-wrapped coffee shop cousins. After dunking in a hot beverage, these home made versions become brownie-like in consistency and even more delicious.

Biscotti

3 eggs, beaten

125g dairy free dark chocolate, chopped into small chunks

200g polenta, plus extra for dusting

50g milled flaxseed, sunflower and pumpkin seed blend

250g crystallised sweetener of choice

1 tsp ground cardamom

3 tbsp gluten and dairy free cocoa powder

½ tsp bicarbonate of soda

1 tsp orange oil

2 tsp chocolate extract

Finely grated zest of 1 orange

½ tsp salt, plus extra for sprinkling

Topping

75g dairy free dark chocolate

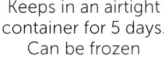

Keeps in an airtight container for 5 days. Can be frozen

TIP

If cardamom does not delight, then we recommend swapping it for 1 teaspoon of espresso coffee granules or ground ginger

WHAT A DELIGHT

Preheat the oven to 170°C / Gas 3.

Line a baking sheet with baking parchment.

Add all of the biscotti ingredients into a bowl and beat with an electric mixer on high speed for 1 minute until well combined.

Dust your hands and work surface with polenta and divide the dough in half. Hand roll each bit of dough into a log shape 7cm wide x 3cm high and place on the baking sheet, spaced apart. Sprinkle the extra salt over the top of each log and place in the fridge to chill for 1 hour.

Transfer the baking sheet with the logs from the fridge to the oven and bake for 20 minutes.

Allow to cool for 10-15 minutes before cutting each log width ways into 1cm slices.

Lay the slices out on the lined baking sheet and bake for 6 minutes before turning them and baking them for a final 6 minutes.

Take them out of the oven and leave on the baking sheet for 5 minutes, and then transfer to a rack to cool.

For the topping, place the chocolate in a microwaveable bowl and melt in the microwave for 30 second bursts on a medium power. Stir the chocolate and repeat, it should take approximately 1 minute.

Then, using a metal spoon, drizzle the chocolate over the cooled biscotti.

Jam Tarts

MAKES 10-12 TARTS
FREE FROM GLUTEN / DAIRY
VEGAN

The beautiful almond pastry elevates these humble tarts to an altogether higher level of deliciousness. The psyllium husk powder is a wonderful binder but can be very expensive. If you prefer not to use it then you will need to "hand squidge" the pastry a bit as it will break up a little when rolling out.

Pastry

50g brown rice flour, plus extra for dusting

100g ground almonds

50ml rapeseed oil, plus extra for brushing

2 tbsp liquid sweetener of choice

¼ tsp of salt

Zest of 1 clementine or small orange

1 tsp psyllium husk powder

Filling

Batch of Half Jam of your choice (see page 197)

Preheat the oven to 150°C / Gas 2.

Brush a tart tin with rapeseed oil.

Pop all of the pastry ingredients into a bowl and beat with an electric mixer on high speed for 1 minute until you have what looks like clumps of fluffy breadcrumbs. Dust your hands with rice flour. Then, by hand, bring the mix together to form a ball of soft slightly sticky pastry.

Wrap the dough in clingfilm and chill for 1 hour.

Dust your hands, rolling pin and work surface with rice flour and roll out the pastry to approximately ¼cm thick. Using a 5cm diameter cutter you should get 10-12 tarts. Pop them into the tart tin.

Spoon 1 heaped teaspoon of jam into each case. The Half Jam does not spread as much as ordinary jam. Bake for 12-15 minutes, or until the pastry is lightly golden. Leave in the tin for 5 minutes and then transfer to a rack to cool.

 Omit the rice flour and ground almonds and replace with 150g of gluten free plain flour.

Keeps in an airtight container for 3 days. Can be frozen

 TIP

For a cheat's lemon meringue you can use dairy free coconut yoghurt and a mini dollop of lemon curd in each case, instead of the jam. No need to bake these toppings

Buried Treasure Garibaldi

MAKES 25 SMALL BISCUITS
FREE FROM GLUTEN / NUTS

We've added a little bit of bejewelled bling to these old fashioned biscuits. Devilishly good when sandwiched with vanilla ice cream.

Biscuits

115g sorghum flour, plus extra for dusting
90g butter, cubed
¼ tsp of salt
35g crystallised sweetener of choice
2 tsp gluten free baking powder
50g Florentine Mix (see page 186)

Topping

1 egg white, beaten
Crystallised sweetener of choice, for sprinkling

Preheat the oven to 180°C / Gas 4.

Line a baking sheet with baking parchment.

To make the biscuit dough, place the sorghum flour, butter, salt, crystallised sweetener and baking powder into a food processor and blitz for 1 minute until a dough forms.

Liberally dust a work surface and rolling pin with sorghum flour. Roll the dough out on the work surface to a rectangle, approximately ¼cm thick. Sprinkle the Florentine Mix over half the surface and then fold the other half on top and roll everything again so you end up with a rectangle approximately 20cm x 30cm. It doesn't matter if the edges are wobbly. Then cut the rolled dough with a knife into fingers or use a cookie cutter.

Space the biscuits out onto the baking sheet, brush each one with the beaten egg white and sprinkle with crystallised sweetener.

Bake for 12 minutes until lightly golden. Leave on the baking sheet for 5 minutes, and transfer with a fish slice to a rack to cool.

Keeps in an airtight container for 7 days. Can be frozen

TIP
Rather than making the Florentine Mix specially, you can use any dried fruits or seeds you have to hand. Toasting the seeds is worthwhile as the flavour is so much more robust

Dorsety Whirls

MAKES 23 SANDWICHED BISCUITS
FREE FROM GLUTEN / NUTS

These melt in the mouth lovelies are our take on Viennese Whirls. We had trouble fending off predators during the photoshoot. If you want to pipe the filling use the butter cream recipe. The cream cheese version works well for spreading rather than piping.

Whirls

250g butter, chilled and diced
50g icing sugar (we used unrefined golden)
250g sorghum flour
50g cornflour
½ tsp vanilla paste
2 egg yolks

Cream cheese or butter cream filling

100g vegetarian cream cheese or softened butter
200g icing sugar (we used unrefined golden)
½ tsp vanilla paste

Finishing

Batch of Half Jam of your choice (see page 197)
Vanilla bean sugar or icing sugar, for dusting

The biscuits (without the filling) will keep in an airtight container for 5 days

TIP

You can try adding crumbled freeze dried raspberries to the biscuit mixture for an intense fruitiness

Ohhh, how lovely!

Preheat the oven to 170°C / Gas 3.

Line a baking sheet with baking parchment.

Put the butter, icing sugar, sorghum flour, cornflour, vanilla paste and egg yolks in a food processor and blitz for 1-2 minutes until a soft dough forms. Spoon the dough into a piping bag fitted with a large star nozzle. Pipe 16 6cm rosettes of the dough onto the lined baking sheet. The Whirls will spread as they bake, so make sure you leave plenty of space between them. Bake in the centre of the oven for 13-15 minutes or until pale golden brown and firm. Leave on the baking sheet for 5 minutes then transfer to a rack to cool completely. Repeat until all the dough is used, to make approximately 46 biscuits.

For the filling, put the cream cheese or butter into a bowl and sift the icing sugar on top. Add the vanilla paste and beat with an electric whisk until light and smooth.

Spoon a little Half Jam onto the flat side of half of the biscuits and place, jam side up, on the cooling rack. Pipe the butter cream or spread the cream cheese filling onto the remaining biscuits and then sandwich them together. Place on a serving plate and sprinkle with the vanilla bean dusting sugar or icing sugar.

Omit the sorghum flour, cornflour and egg yolks and replace with 300g of gluten free plain flour.

Extra Lemony Cakelets

MAKES 12 CAKELETS
FREE FROM GLUTEN

There is a veritable team stampede for these as soon as the oven timer "pings". A very pleasurable way of loading up on one's RDA of vitamin C.

Cakelets

140g crystallised sweetener of choice

70g sorghum flour

1½ tsp gluten free baking powder

25g ground golden flaxseed

¼ tsp vanilla paste

70g ground almonds

2 eggs

175g butter, melted

2 tsp lemon oil

Zest of 2 lemons (reserve the zested, whole lemons for the drench)

35g lemon curd

Drench

50g crystallised sweetener of choice

Juice of 2 lemons

1 tbsp crystallised sweetener of choice, for sprinkling

Preheat the oven to 170°C / Gas 3.

Line a 12 hole muffin pan with paper muffin cases.

Place all the cakelet ingredients into a bowl and beat with an electric mixer on high speed for 1 minute until well combined.

Spoon this mixture evenly between the cases, filling them three quarters full to avoid the cakelets spilling over. Bake for 18-20 minutes until they are springy to the touch.

To make the drench, melt the crystallised sweetener with the lemon juice in the microwave for 30 seconds on full power. Whilst still hot from the oven, prick each cakelet deeply with a cake skewer or cocktail stick several times. Pour a share of the drench over each cakelet. Sprinkle with crystallised sweetener to finish.

Transfer the cakelets from the muffin pan to a wire rack to cool.

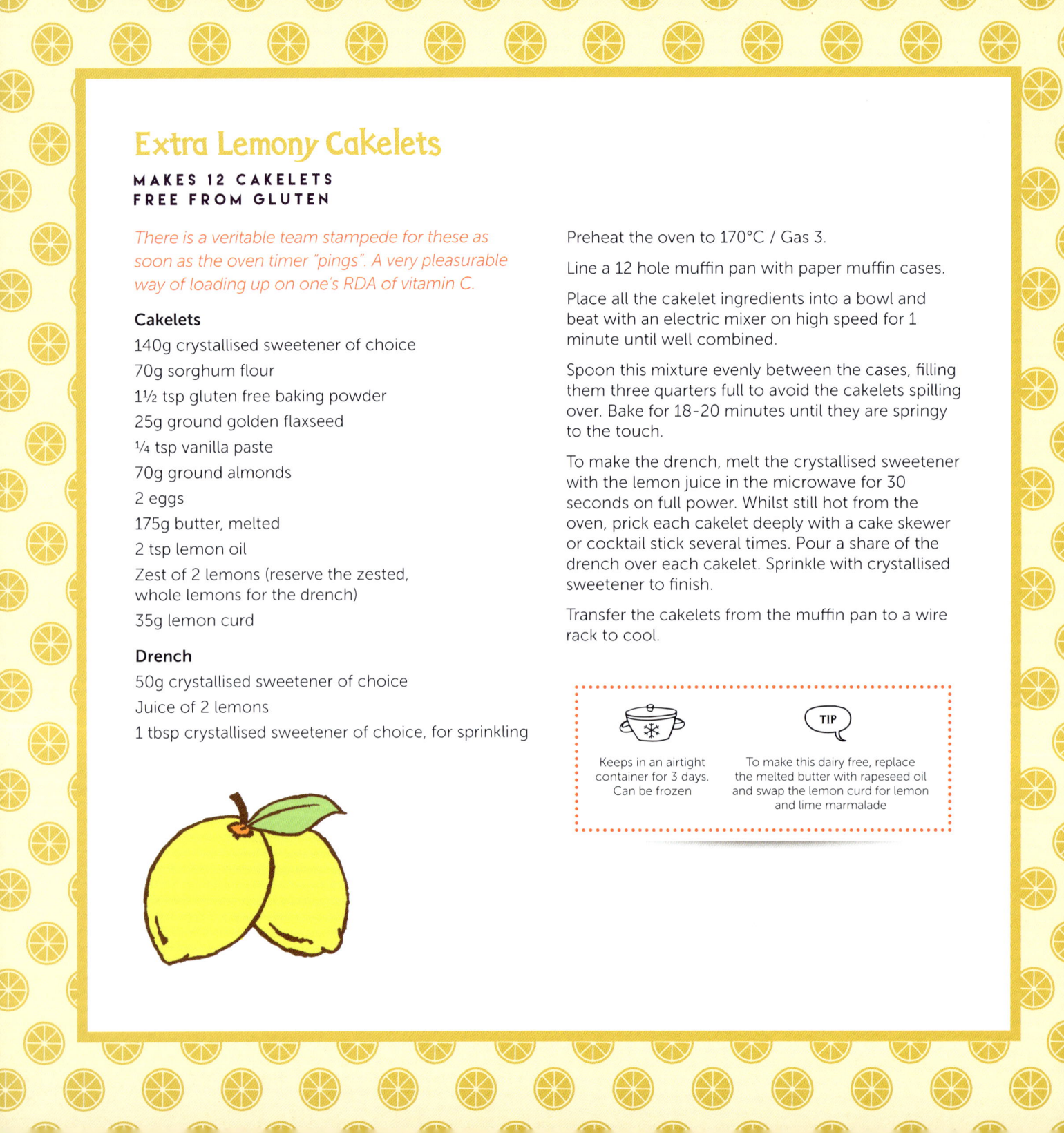

Keeps in an airtight container for 3 days. Can be frozen

TIP

To make this dairy free, replace the melted butter with rapeseed oil and swap the lemon curd for lemon and lime marmalade

Mog's Raspberry Buns

MAKES 18-20 BUNS
FREE FROM GLUTEN / DAIRY

This is an adaptation of my mum's legendary rock cake recipe. The Half Jam (see page 197) is pleasingly tart and ridiculously easy to make.

Buns

200g ground almonds

100g sorghum flour

100g polenta

165g crystallised sweetener of choice

½ tsp salt

½ tsp vanilla paste

230ml rapeseed oil

3 eggs

Finely grated zest of 1 lemon

2 tsp gluten free baking powder

½ tsp bicarbonate of soda

Finishing

Half a batch of Raspberry Half Jam (see page 197)

Preheat the oven to 170°C / Gas 3.

Line a baking sheet with baking parchment.

For the buns, place all the ingredients into a bowl and combine using an electric mixer on a high speed for 1 minute until a soft dough is formed.

Form 18-20 balls of dough, approximately 50g each, with 2 metal spoons. The aim is to create rough, rock like shapes. Place them on the baking sheet. The buns will spread as they bake, so make sure you leave plenty of space between them.

Make a well in each bun with your thumb. Spoon 1 teaspoon of the Half Jam into each well.

Bake for 16-18 minutes until firm to the touch and lightly golden. Leave on the baking sheet for 5 minutes then transfer to a rack to cool completely.

Omit the ground almonds, sorghum flour, polenta, gluten free baking powder and bicarbonate of soda and replace with 400g gluten free self-raising flour.

 **Keeps in an airtight container for 3 days. Can be frozen**

 TIP We've kept the bun mixture plain and simple but you could add toasted seeds, dried fruit or nuts as you wish

IF YOU HAVE TOO MUCH ROASTED BUTTERNUT SQUASH SIMPLY FREEZE IT FOR YOUR NEXT BATCH OF THIS CAKE.

New England Loaf

MAKES 1 TRAYBAKE OR 1 X 900G LOAF
FREE FROM GLUTEN

This cake truly delivers on taste and texture. The roasting of the squash is a step not to be skipped as it really does add depth of flavour. Perfect with a mid morning brew.

Loaf

Rapeseed oil, for brushing

Approximately ¼ butternut squash, peeled and chopped, (around 165g cooked weight)

1 tsp ground cinnamon

3 eggs

125g crystallised sweetener of choice

100g shelled hemp

60g sorghum flour

1½ tsp gluten free baking powder

½ tsp bicarbonate of soda

125g crunchy peanut butter

150g milk chocolate buttons

Topping

25g milk chocolate buttons

25g dark chocolate buttons

25g white chocolate buttons

40g peanuts (use salted if you wish), chopped and toasted

Sea salt, for sprinkling

Keeps in an airtight container for 3 days. Can be frozen

To make this dairy free, just use dairy free dark chocolate inside the cake and for the topping

Preheat the oven to 200°C / Gas 6.

Brush the traybake or loaf tin with rapeseed oil and line with baking parchment.

Place the butternut squash in a roasting tin and sprinkle with cinnamon. Roast for 25 minutes, stirring half way through the cooking time to prevent sticking. The butternut squash can be prepared and roasted the day before if required.

Reduce the oven to 170°C / Gas 3 if you're baking a traybake, or 150°C / Gas 2 if baking a loaf.

Place the eggs, crystallised sweetener, shelled hemp, sorghum flour, baking powder, bicarbonate of soda and peanut butter into a bowl and beat with an electric mixer on high speed for 1 minute until smooth and well combined. Using a spatula, stir the chocolate buttons and butternut squash into the mixture. Spoon and spread the mixture evenly into the traybake or loaf tin.

Bake the traybake for 25 minutes, or 1 hour 15 minutes if using the loaf tin, until springy to the touch. Leave the cake to cool completely before removing from the tin.

For the topping, melt the milk, dark and white chocolate buttons separately in the microwave for 15 second bursts on medium power. Stir the chocolate and repeat; it should take approximately 30 seconds to 1 minute for the chocolate to melt.

Using the end of a metal spoon, drizzle the melted milk chocolate over the traybake or loaf. Sprinkle with the toasted peanuts and drizzle the dark and white chocolate on top. Finish by sprinkling with sea salt. Allow the chocolate to set before slicing.

Omit the shelled hemp, sorghum flour, baking powder and bicarbonate of soda and replace with 165g gluten free self-raising flour. This cooks 5 minutes quicker than the hemp and sorghum flour recipe.

Real Gingerbread Men

**MAKES ABOUT 25 SMALL MEN USING
A 6CM X 4.5CM SMALL MAN CUTTER
FREE FROM GLUTEN / DAIRY / NUTS**

*Inspired by an old Lebkuchen recipe, we ramped up
the spices resulting in gingerbread men with a little bit
of attitude. We opted for plain and simple icing for the
photoshoot but feel free to go wild... just remember to
send us your pics!*

Gingerbread

175g dark muscovado sugar

125g milled flaxseed, sunflower and pumpkin seed blend

225g sorghum flour, plus extra for dusting

2 tsp ground cinnamon

4 tsp ground ginger

½ tsp bicarbonate of soda

1-2 grinds of black pepper

1 egg

150g runny honey

75g black treacle

80g crystallised or glacé ginger, chopped

Icing

1 egg white, or the equivalent amount of liquid
pasteurised egg white

1 tsp lemon juice

½ tsp vanilla extract

185g icing sugar, sieved (we used golden unrefined)

Finishing

Approximately 20 pink peppercorns

Preheat the oven to 180°C / Gas 4.

Line a baking sheet with baking parchment.

Place all the dry gingerbread ingredients, except the chopped
crystallised ginger, into a food processor and then add the
egg, honey and treacle. Placing the ingredients in this order
means you end with less of a sticky mess to clear up. Blitz
until the mixture binds together. This will take less than 1
minute. The colour darkens slightly in the processor when it
is ready. Then stir the ginger in with a spatula.

Wrap the dough in cling film and chill in the fridge for at
least 1 hour.

Pop a sheet of baking parchment on a work surface and
dust the baking parchment and your hands with sorghum
flour. Split the dough into thirds so that rolling it out is
easier to manage. Dust all 3 portions of dough liberally with
sorghum flour. The trick is to ensure each portion of dough
is thoroughly covered all over with sorghum flour prior to
rolling out. Place the first portion of dough onto the baking
parchment. Place another sheet of baking parchment on
top of the dough and squidge it down a bit with your hands
before rolling out with the rolling pin. You'll need to roll the
dough out to approximately 1cm thickness. To prevent the
dough from sticking to the paper you need to keep dusting
the dough with sorghum flour. Peel off and discard the top
sheet of baking parchment before cutting out your shapes
using your chosen cookie cutter. This bit can be tricky
as the dough is sticky. Try dipping your cookie cutter in
sorghum flour and you will need to peel each man carefully
away from the cutter. Using a fish slice, transfer your men
onto the lined baking sheet, spaced well apart. Repeat this
process with the other 2 portions of dough.

Bake for 8-12 minutes until they are springy to the touch and
darkened slightly on the edges. Leave to cool for 5 minutes
before transferring with a fish slice to a cooling rack.

Continued overleaf...

Allow the gingerbread men to cool completely.

To make the icing, whisk the egg white until you have stiff peaks. Add the lemon juice and vanilla extract. Slowly add the icing sugar, a bit at a time, and beat with an electric mixer on high speed until stiff peaks form again. Decant into an icing bag with a fine plain nozzle. This makes plenty of icing so don't be surprised if you have a surplus. This can be kept in the fridge and warmed through in the microwave when you need it again.

Pipe your icing on as you like and finish off using pink peppercorns for buttons.

 *Omit the milled seed blend, bicarbonate of soda and sorghum flour and replace with 350g gluten free self-raising flour.*

 Keep in an airtight container for 7 days. Can be frozen

 TIP If you prefer a biscuit with a little more "chew" roll out to 1.5cm in thickness and keep the baking time and temperature the same

Retro Chocolate Oat Delight

MAKES 1 TRAYBAKE
FREE FROM GLUTEN / NUTS

This harks back to my school canteen circa 1989. After the compulsory cross country running we'd skip lunch (naughty) and fill our boots with this devilishly moreish pud. We've since added the cherries for a touch of post 1980s sophistication.

Oat Delight
250g butter

175g liquid sweetener of choice

350g gluten free oats

115g dried sour cherries

2 tbsp cocoa powder

Topping
250g dark chocolate

1 tbsp rapeseed oil

Preheat the oven to 170°C / Gas 3.

Line the traybake tin with baking parchment.

Combine the butter and liquid sweetener together in a pan on a medium heat. Place the oats, cherries and cocoa powder into a bowl and sift with a fork. Add the melted butter and liquid sweetener to the oat mixture, and using a wooden spoon, mix well.

Spoon the mixture into the tin and spread evenly, pushing into the corners. The surface should be reasonably smooth. Bake for 15 minutes until lightly golden. Leave in the tin to cool completely.

For the topping, place the chocolate and rapeseed oil in a microwaveable bowl and melt in the microwave for 30 second bursts on medium power. Stir and repeat. It should take approximately 1½-2 minutes.

Pour the melted topping over the cooled traybake, spreading the topping to the edges with a palette knife, tapping the tray to remove any air pockets from the chocolate. Chill until the chocolate has set, then cut and devour.

Keeps in an airtight container for 5 days. Can be frozen

TIP
To go dairy free switch from butter to virgin coconut oil and use dairy free cocoa and dark chocolate

SCRUMMY
SUPPERS

Lasagne, pizza, tarts & more

Around the table
for family time,
supper is here
and like kings
we shall dine

Gnocchi, Cheese & Tomato Bake

MAKES 1 X 30CM X 25CM OVENPROOF DISH
FREE FROM GLUTEN / NUTS

We use King Edward potatoes for a lovely smooth textured gnocchi. The richness of the cheese sauce is offset by the capers and the slightly tangy layer of tomato sauce. A really great autumn and winter supper dish.

Gnocchi

500g potatoes, peeled and cut into evenly sized pieces

¼ tsp salt

75g tapioca flour, plus extra for dusting'

75g potato flour

1 egg, beaten with a fork

Cheese sauce

½ pint milk

1 tbsp cornflour

¼ tsp ground white pepper

75g vegetarian mature cheddar, grated

1 tsp wholegrain mustard

100g shallots, roasted until softened and if large, roughly chopped

100g cherry tomatoes, halved

2 tbsp capers, chopped

Base

Batch of Charlotte's Tomato Sauce (see page 194)

Topping

25g vegetarian Italian hard cheese, finely grated

Keeps in the fridge for 3 days

TIP
If you're short on time try either ready made gluten free gnocchi or gluten free pasta

Preheat the oven to 180°C / Gas 4.

Boil the potatoes for 20 minutes. Strain, then leave for a couple minutes to dry and cool in a colander.

Either put the potatoes through a potato ricer or mash them. Place the riced or mashed potato on a clean dry tea towel, wrap the towel around the potato and squeeze any moisture out. The aim is to have as little moisture in the potato as possible. The less moisture, the lighter the gnocchi.

Pop the potato, salt, tapioca flour, potato flour and the egg into a bowl and mix well with a wooden spoon until a loose dough is formed.

Dust a dry, clean work surface with tapioca flour. Place the dough onto the work surface and knead it by hand for 1-2 minutes, until a smooth dough has formed. Be careful not to over knead. Do not be tempted to add flour at this point. Too much flour will result in hard gnocchi.

Divide the dough into 4 pieces. Dust a rolling pin with tapioca flour. Roll each piece into a long sausage shape about 3cm in diameter. Cut each sausage shape into small pieces about 3cm long. Dip a fork into some of the tapioca flour, then using the back of the fork, press and slightly flatten each piece of gnocchi, leaving line marks.

To cook, use a dry pastry brush to dust off any excess flour from the gnocchi and place into a large pot of boiling water, a few at a time. Cook the gnocchi until they float to the top, this will take about 2-3 minutes. Gently remove the cooked gnocchi with a slotted spoon, and drain thoroughly while continuing to cook the rest of them.

For the cheese sauce, bring the milk to the boil in a pan. In a small bowl mix the cornflour with a little cold water, using just enough to make a paste. Whisk this paste quickly into the hot milk, it will then thicken pretty instantly. Simmer this mixture for 1 minute on a low heat, and add the pepper, cheddar, mustard, roasted shallots, cherry tomatoes and capers. Whilst still on the low heat, whisk the sauce again until the cheese has melted. Remove from the heat and set to one side.

Place Charlotte's Tomato Sauce into the bottom of the ovenproof dish and place the gnocchi evenly on top. Pour the cheese sauce over and sprinkle with the Italian hard cheese. Bake for 30-35 minutes or until bubbling and crispy golden on the top. Serve hot.

Vibrant Veggie Stack

MAKES 6 STACKS
FREE FROM GLUTEN / NUTS

These are beautiful, tasty towers packed full of nutrients. Very easy to assemble and the bean bases can be used with all manner of toppings. King Edward's are our ideal potato to use here, as they mash well.

Topping

2 red peppers, deseeded and cut into chunky strips

1 butternut squash, peeled, deseeded and cut into 6 chunky discs

Rapeseed oil, for roasting

Batch of Tomato, Red Pepper & Pumpkin Seed Tapenade (see page 183)

170g Capricorn goats cheese (2 packs)

3 tbsp fresh thyme, chopped

3 tsp cracked black pepper

Batch of Peasto (see page 181)

Base

4 medium potatoes, peeled, grated and squeezed in a tea towel to remove any excess liquid

400g tinned butter beans, drained and lightly mashed with a fork

115g butter, melted

4 sprigs fresh thyme, chopped

¼ tsp salt

4-5 tbsp rapeseed oil, for frying

Preheat the oven to 200°C / Gas 6.

To make the topping, roast the red peppers and butternut squash in a roasting tin with a little rapeseed oil for 20-25 minutes. Once cooked, allow to cool.

To make the base, place the potato, butter beans, butter, thyme and salt into a bowl and beat with an electric mixer on high speed for 1 minute until well combined. Divide the mixture evenly into 6 portions and by hand, mould into patties 9cm diameter, and roughly 2½cm thick.

Place 1 tablespoon of rapeseed oil in a pan on a high heat. Once the oil is hot, cook 2-3 patties at a time until they are crispy and golden on both sides. It will take 3-4 minutes to cook each side. Avoid putting the patties in the pan before it is hot or they will go soggy. You will need to add a little bit of oil each time you add patties to the pan. Set to one side to cool.

To assemble each stack, spread the Tomato, Red Pepper & Pumpkin Seed Tapenade generously over each cooled butter bean base.

Place a disc of roasted butternut squash onto each of the bases and top with roasted red pepper. Slice each goats cheese into thirds and lay one over the top of each stack. Sprinkle thyme and pepper over the top and drizzle with the Peasto.

Best eaten on the day

 TIP

If you're short on time, shop bought red pepper tapenade and a good vegetarian pesto can be used instead of making your own

Spinach & Ricotta Lasagne

MAKES 1 X 30CM X 25CM OVENPROOF DISH
FREE FROM GLUTEN / NUTS

This is a lovely pasta to work with and you can roll it out with ease. The filling is full to bursting with fresh herbs and lends itself to adaptation depending on the herbs you have to hand.

Pasta

150g tapioca flour

125g milled flaxseed, sunflower and pumpkin seed blend

125g cornflour

½ tsp salt

2 tbsp olive oil

4 eggs

1 tbsp tomato puree

Filling

500g mushrooms, sliced

Olive oil, for drizzling

½ tsp ground nutmeg

400g spinach leaves, washed and dried

1 tbsp cracked black pepper

6 fresh sage leaves, snipped

Finely grated zest of 1 lemon

500g tub ricotta

4 tbsp Peasto (see page 181)

Topping

75g vegetarian Italian hard cheese, grated

35g pumpkin seeds, toasted

Keeps in the fridge for 3 days. Can be frozen

TIP
You can also add fresh chopped herbs to the pasta ingredients

Preheat the oven to 180°C / Gas 4.

Brush the ovenproof dish with olive oil.

Pop all of the pasta ingredients into a food processor and blitz for 1 minute until a dough is formed. Liberally dust a work surface and your hands with tapioca flour. Knead the dough gently with your hands until smooth and lump free. Divide the dough into 3 pieces and roll out each piece onto sheets of baking parchment cut to the size of the ovenproof dish. The idea is you can then easily transfer the pasta sheets to the ovenproof dish by placing the pasta in position and then peeling off the baking parchment.

Place the mushrooms in a large frying pan on a medium heat. Drizzle the mushrooms with olive oil, add the nutmeg and then mix together to coat the mushrooms. Fry the mushrooms for 5-6 minutes or until they start to soften and colour up. Add the spinach and keep moving them around until they wilt and mix in with the mushrooms. This will take up to 1 minute. Add the pepper, sage leaves and lemon zest. Stir and then remove from the heat.

Lay 1 of the pasta sheets on the bottom of the ovenproof dish. On top of the pasta sheet spoon half of the mushroom mixture, dollop a quarter of the ricotta in blobs over the mushrooms and then dot with half of the Peasto. Place another pasta sheet on top and add another mushroom, ricotta and Peasto layer.

Place the final pasta sheet on and spread the remaining half of ricotta over the top. Sprinkle with the Italian hard cheese and pumpkin seeds, and bake for 30-35 minutes until bubbling and mid golden in colour.

Tian with Courgette, Blue Vinny & Sweet Potato

MAKES 1 X 20CM CASSEROLE DISH
FREE FROM GLUTEN / NUTS

Being a huge fan of the great and late Elizabeth David, I was inspired by her recipe for a courgette tian which I discovered many years ago. A tian is the name for the provencal earthenware pot that this dish is traditionally cooked in. The dish is a cross between a soufflé and a Spanish omelette, and is a super easy, economical way to use up vegetables slightly past their best. It's also utterly delicious.

1 medium sweet potato, peeled and cut into chunky sections

3 tbsp olive oil

3 cloves garlic, chopped

1 courgette, sliced

½ tsp of salt

½ tsp cracked black pepper

6 eggs

Fresh thyme, stems removed and snipped

100g vegetarian mature cheddar, grated

100g Dorset Blue Vinny or vegetarian Stilton, crumbled

Topping

75g vegetarian mature cheddar, grated

Preheat the oven to 200°C / Gas 6.

Parboil the sweet potato for 4-5 minutes and drain. Once cooled cut into ½cm thick slices.

Pop the olive oil into the casserole dish and add the garlic, courgette, salt and pepper. Mix well with your hands. Place in the oven for 10 minutes.

Place the eggs with the thyme, cheddar and Blue Vinny or Stilton into a bowl and beat with an electric mixer on high speed for 1 minute. The ingredients need to be well combined and it should be slightly frothy.

Take the casserole dish containing the courgette mixture out of the oven.

Reduce the oven to 180°C / Gas 4

Place the sweet potato slices on top of the courgette mixture. Pour the beaten egg mixture over the top and finally sprinkle with the extra cheddar.

Bake for 30-35 minutes until puffed up and mid dark golden brown in colour. Serve warm.

Best eaten hot from the oven

Serve with a lightly toasted bread, such as the Seeded Loaf (see page 51)

Spicy Bean Balls
with spaghetti & Charlotte's Tomato Sauce

MAKES 16-20 BALLS
FREE FROM GLUTEN / DAIRY / NUTS
VEGAN

The spicy bean balls and tomato sauce are knock-outs in terms of flavour. Believing in honesty being the best policy, I'm not sure that homemade gluten free spaghetti necessarily warrants the effort involved. From our experience it's extremely hard to create something that doesn't break off into shorter sections. We rate Heinz gluten free spaghetti, which is widely available.

Spicy Bean Balls

1 tbsp rapeseed oil

2 cloves garlic, finely chopped

1 onion, finely chopped

140g red peppers, finely chopped

400g tinned butter beans, rinsed and drained

400g tinned black eyed beans, rinsed and drained

1 red chilli, finely chopped

1 tsp cumin seeds, toasted

3 tbsp pumpkin seeds, toasted

½ tsp salt

2 tsp cracked black pepper

25g gluten free oats

1 tsp chilli flakes

½ tsp chilli powder

2 tbsp of curly or flat leaf parsley, chopped

200g tinned kidney beans, rinsed, drained and lightly mashed

Gluten free flour, for dusting

Spaghetti

4 servings of shop bought gluten free spaghetti.
Serving size as per packet guidelines

Finishing

Batch of Charlotte's Tomato Sauce (see page 194)

Preheat the oven to 180°C / Gas 4.

Line a baking sheet with baking parchment.

Warm 1 tablespoon of rapeseed oil in a frying pan on a medium heat. Add the garlic, onion and red peppers and fry until softened. This will take 4-5 minutes. Remove from the heat and set aside.

Place all the Spicy Bean Ball ingredients, except the kidney beans, into a food processor and blitz for up to 30 seconds until everything is finely chopped, but not pulverized. You're aiming for some texture. Decant this mixture into a mixing bowl and then add the lightly mashed kidney beans and mix in gently with a fork.

Dust your hands with flour and shape the mixture into golf ball sized balls.

Evenly space the balls on the baking sheet and bake for 12 minutes until they are golden brown in colour.

Whilst the balls are in the oven, prepare the spaghetti as per the instructions on the packet. Towards the end of the spaghetti and bean ball cooking time, warm Charlotte's Tomato Sauce in a pan on a medium heat for 4-5 minutes.

Dish out the spaghetti, place the bean balls on top and spoon over the sauce.

Bean Balls keep in the fridge for 3 days. Can be frozen

TIP The Bean Balls also work really well served with houmous and a salad if you're after a lighter bite

Cheddar, Tomato & Red Onion Tartlets

**MAKES 6 X 10CM LOOSE BOTTOMED
TART TINS
FREE FROM GLUTEN / NUTS**

*Such a classic flavour combination, these never fail to
delight. Gorgeous served as a simple supper along side
the Celeriac, Sage and Hazelnut Bake (see page 116) and
a simple leaf salad.*

Pastry

Vegetable oil, for brushing

140g brown rice flour, plus extra for dusting

75g cornflour

½ tsp chilli powder

1 tsp sweet smoked paprika

60g butter, chilled and cubed

2 eggs

Filling

125g passata

90g red onion, roasted and diced

300g vegetarian mature cheddar, grated

18 pieces Oven Roasted Tomatoes (see page 195)

3 tbsp fresh basil, chopped

Keeps in the fridge
for 3 days.
Can be frozen

TIP

You can add wholegrain mustard to the filling
if you fancy a bit of a bite. Halved cherry
tomatoes can be substituted for the Oven
Roasted Tomatoes if you prefer

Preheat the oven to 170°C / Gas 3.

Brush the tart tins with vegetable oil.

Weigh out all dry ingredients for the pastry into a food
processor and add the butter. Blitz until the mix resembles
breadcrumbs and there are no lumps of butter. From time
to time stop and make sure no dry mix is left in the bottom.
Then add the eggs and continue to blitz.

Mix until the ingredients clump together and forms a soft
pastry dough. If the mix is a little dry or not clumping
together you may need to add a little cold water. Pour this
in a little at a time with the mixer running - be careful not to
make it too wet and sticky.

Liberally dust your hands with brown rice flour. Evenly
divide the pastry into 6 portions, hand roll them into balls
and dust them with brown rice flour. Hand mould each ball
into a disc approximately 1-2cm thick, and press these discs
gently into the tart tins. You will need to squidge the pastry
using your fingertips to fit around the sides of each tart tin.

Space the tartlets out on a baking sheet. Bake for 18-20
minutes until the pastry feels firm and is light golden brown.
Once out of the oven, allow to cool completely before
adding the filling.

Evenly distribute the passata into each tartlet, then add
the roasted red onion, cheddar, and top with 3 pieces of
tomato. Sprinkle with basil.

Bake the filled tarts for approximately 20 minutes. The
cheese should be bubbling and mid golden brown in colour.

Serve either warm or cold.

Chilli Con Veggie
with Elaine's Oregano Cobblings

MAKES 1 X 20CM CASSEROLE DISH
FREE FROM GLUTEN / DAIRY / NUTS
VEGAN

This is a super easy recipe. I'd recommend buying a specially blended spice mix though. They're put together by chilli aficionados who really know their stuff. There are lots of suppliers online; we use chillipepperpete.com You can, of course, use your own spices and I've suggested a mix for you to do yourself.

The cobblings are our invention and are a cross between the drier cobbler and the wetter dumpling. At Honeybuns, opinion is divided on how to cook them. Elaine, our head baker, puts it like this, "For the proper soggy bottom, the cobblings need to be half submerged in the chilli for the whole cooking time." Personally, I prefer a crisper bottom. I like to bake them separately and then just pop them on a side plate to accompany the chilli. Horses for courses as they say.

This is even better after an overnighter in the fridge. Keeps in the fridge for 3 days. Can be frozen

TIP

The cobblings are lovely but you could substitute for a bowl of wild rice instead, served with a wedge of lime

Roast veggies

1 red pepper

1 red onion

1 red chilli

150g cherry tomatoes

100g mushrooms

1 tbsp olive oil

Spices and seasonings

2 tsp cracked black pepper

1 tsp hot chilli powder

½ tsp dried oregano

½ tsp cumin seeds, crushed

Chilli sauce

400g tinned chopped tomatoes

200g tinned butter beans, drained

200g tinned kidney beans, drained

200g tinned black eyed beans, drained

100ml vegan red wine

2 tbsp sun dried tomato paste

1 tbsp crystallised sweetener of choice

1 tbsp capsicum chutney- we love English Provender

Tabasco, to taste (we use several dashes)

Vegetarian and gluten free Worcestershire sauce, to taste

Elaine's Oregano Cobblings

70g sorghum flour

50g gluten, dairy free and vegan suet

25g tapioca flour

2 tbsp fresh oregano, chopped

2 tbsp fresh mint, chopped

½ tsp bicarbonate of soda

½ tsp cream of tartar

½ tsp salt

½ tsp cracked black pepper

1 tsp dried chilli flakes (optional)

75-100ml coconut milk

Preheat the oven to 180°C / Gas 4.

Line a baking sheet with baking parchment.

To prepare the roast veggies, chop the pepper, onion, chilli, tomatoes and mushrooms (1cm pieces are fine). You can deseed the chilli or leave them in if you want a bit of a kick. Pop them into a roasting tray with the spices and seasonings and drizzle with the olive oil. Roast the vegetables for 20 minutes.

Pop the chilli sauce ingredients and spiced roasted veggies into a lidded casserole dish and mix with a wooden spoon or spatula until all the ingredients are combined.

Place all of the cobbling ingredients except the coconut milk into a large bowl and mix well using an electric hand mixer on high speed for 1 minute. Add the coconut milk gradually to bind into a soft elastic dough. You may not need to use all of the milk. The mixture will seem sloppy to start with and then will suddenly thicken.

Divide the mixture into 6 pieces and form into dumpling shapes on the baking sheet.

You have two options with the cobblings. You can bake the cobblings separately ahead of time for 20 minutes. This creates a lovely slightly crisp outside with a soft centre. Pop them on top of the chilli for the last 5 minutes of baking time.

Or you can pop them on the top of the chilli and cook them together.

Finally pop the lid on the casserole dish to prevent the chilli drying out and bake for 40 minutes (with or without the cobblings). Serve piping hot from the oven.

Roast Artichoke Pizza

MAKES 1 X LARGE PIZZA TO SHARE (OR BE A GLEEFUL GLUTTON FOR THE NIGHT)
FREE FROM GLUTEN / NUTS

This is a really easy base to work with and it's also a fab vehicle to transport hidden vegetables to unsuspecting tummies. This is one of my favourite toppings but you can run amok as your fancy takes you. As the base is mostly made of cheese, you may want to counterbalance this with less cheese on the topping.

Pizza base

250g vegetarian mozzarella

2 eggs

115g vegetarian cream cheese

115g sorghum flour, plus extra for dusting

100g spinach, watercress or rocket leaves, washed and dried

50g vegetarian Italian hard cheese, grated

3 tsp dried Italian herb mix

Topping

1 tsp cracked black pepper

3 tbsp Peasto (see page 181)

280g jar artichokes in oil, drained but keep the oil in reserve

A few mushrooms, thinly sliced, enough to cover the pizza

1 tbsp fresh oregano leaves

1 tbsp capers

1 tbsp pine nuts, toasted

Vegetarian Italian hard cheese shavings, to taste

Preheat the oven to 180°C / Gas 4.

Line a baking sheet with baking parchment.

Place all the pizza base ingredients in a food processor and blitz until a sticky dough is formed. Liberally dust your hands with sorghum flour to handle the dough. Remove the dough from the food processor, wrap it in clingfilm and chill it in the fridge for at least 30 minutes.

Spread the chilled dough onto the baking sheet. With a palette knife or back of a spoon spread the dough into a 25cm thin circle - we like them thin and have based cooking times on skinny. Just remember to bake for longer if you want a thicker base.

Sprinkle cracked black pepper over the top.

Bake for 8-10 minutes. It will be just starting to turn golden, especially around the edges.

Remove from the oven and leave on the tray to cool. Take care as the base is quite fragile at this stage.

In a small bowl mix the Peasto with 2 tablespoon of the reserved artichoke oil using a fork. You're aiming for a runny solution which you can brush over the pizza base.

Using a pastry brush, spread the Peasto mix over the pizza base.

Scatter the artichokes and mushrooms over the pizza base. Drizzle lightly with more of the tasty oil from the artichokes and sprinkle with oregano, capers, toasted pine nuts, Italian hard cheese shavings and pepper.

Bake for 8-10 minutes until the mushrooms are just turning lightly golden.

The pizza with topping keeps in the fridge for 2 days. Reheat gently before eating. Bases can be frozen

TIP

Try roasted tomatoes and wilted spinach as an alternative topping

A delightful supper to snuggle up with

Mog's Mousakka

MAKES 1 X 30CM X 25CM OVENPROOF DISH
FREE FROM GLUTEN / NUTS

Growing up next door to an Anglo-Greek family, I remember going around to their house with my mum on 'Moussaka Day'. My mum had a lesson in how to make it and then set about growing her own aubergines in the greenhouse. This is perfect comfort food, ideal for once the evenings start to draw in and thoughts turn to "snuggle up suppers".

Roasted aubergines
Olive oil, for brushing

2 aubergines (raw weight approximately 500g)

1 tsp cumin seeds

Mince and tomato filling
300g frozen gluten free vegetarian mince

2 large tomatoes, chopped

1 red onion, chopped

3 tsp fresh oregano, chopped

2 tsp capers

400g passata or chopped tomatoes

Vegetarian and gluten free Worcestershire sauce, to taste

½ tsp cracked black pepper

2 tbsp olive oil

3 tsp fresh thyme, chopped

3 tbsp pitted black olives, chopped

½ tsp fennel seeds

10 fresh mint leaves, chopped

100ml red wine

White sauce
4 eggs

200g Greek yoghurt

100g crème fraiche

75g vegetarian Italian hard cheese, grated

Topping
350g fresh vegetarian mozzarella, sliced

Approximately 50g vegetarian Italian hard cheese, finely grated

1 tsp cumin seeds

Preheat the oven to 180°C / Gas 4.

Brush a roasting tin with olive oil. Line a baking sheet with baking parchment.

Wash, top and tail the aubergines and slice them lengthways. Aim for slices approximately 2½cm thick. Brush the slices with olive oil and sprinkle with cumin seeds. Pop them on the baking sheet and put in the oven for 20 minutes. Turn the slices and brush them again with olive oil after 10 minutes. Keep the cumin seeds on the sheet - it doesn't matter if they fall underneath the aubergines.

Pop all the ingredients for the mince and tomato filling into the roasting tin and place in the oven for 25 minutes.

Place the white sauce ingredients into a mixing bowl and beat with an electric hand mixer on high speed for 1 minute until combined.

To assemble the moussaka, cover the bottom of your ovenproof dish with the sliced aubergines - tip out and use all the cumin seeds too. Spread the mince and tomato filling over the aubergines and pour the white sauce over the top. To finish, add the sliced mozzarella and sprinkle with Italian hard cheese and cumin seeds.

Bake for 40-45 minutes until the topping turns a golden colour and bubbles around the edges and the white sauce has set. Serve whilst still piping hot.

Keeps in the fridge for 3 days (it improves after a day or two). Can be frozen

You can use butternut squash instead of aubergine - just slice it to half the thickness as it takes a bit longer to cook. You can add peas to the mince mix too - delicious

Carrot, Almond & Coriander Tartlet

See overleaf for this recipe

Carrot, Almond & Coriander Tartlets

**MAKES 6 X 10CM LOOSE BOTTOMED
TART TINS**
FREE FROM GLUTEN / DAIRY / NUTS

*This classic flavour combination tastes really fresh and is
a great dairy free lunch or supper solution. We present
these tartlets on a board surrounded by various tapenades
(see page 182). We also use multi-coloured carrots when
available, as in the photograph, for extra visual oomph.*

Pastry

Vegetable oil, for brushing

140g brown rice flour, plus extra for dusting

75g cornflour

1 tsp chilli powder

1 tsp smoked paprika

60g vegetable margarine, chilled

2 eggs

Filling

200g Chantenay carrots

Rapeseed oil, for drizzling

35g whole almonds, toasted

¼ tsp salt

¼ tsp ground white pepper

2 tbsp fresh coriander, chopped

2 tsp coriander seeds, toasted

125g coconut cream

1 small egg

Topping

12 Chantenay carrots, topped and tailed

Fresh coriander, chopped, for sprinkling

Keeps in the fridge for 3
days. Can be frozen

TIP

Parsnips can be used instead
of carrots if you prefer

Preheat the oven to 170°C / Gas 3.

Brush the tart tins with vegetable oil.

Weigh out all the dry ingredients for the pastry into a
food processor and add the margarine. Blitz until the mix
resembles breadcrumbs, this will take about 1 minute. From
time to time stop and make sure no dry mix is left in the
bottom. Then add the eggs and continue to blitz. Mix until
the ingredients clump together and forms a soft pastry
dough. If the mix is a little dry or not clumping together you
may need to add a little cold water. Pour this in a little at a
time with the mixer running - be careful not to make it too
wet and sticky.

Liberally dust your hands with brown rice flour. Evenly divide
the pastry into 6 portions, hand roll them into balls and dust
them with brown rice flour. Hand mould each ball into a disc
approximately 1-2cm thick, and press these discs gently into
the tart tins. You will need to squidge the pastry using your
fingertips to fit around the sides of each tart tin.

Space the tartlets out on a baking sheet. Bake for 18-20
minutes until the pastry feels firm and is light golden brown.
Once out of the oven, allow to cool completely before
adding the filling.

Increase the oven to 200°C / Gas 6.

For the filling, place the carrots in a roasting tin. Drizzle them
with rapeseed oil and roast for 20 minutes. You can roast the
12 additional carrots for the topping at the same time. Once
cooled, place the 12 carrots for the topping to one side.
Place the carrots for the filling in a food processor with the
remaining filling ingredients and blitz for 1-2 minutes until a
smooth paste is formed. Spoon the filling evenly between the
tartlets; you can heap them up quite high.

For the topping, slice each of the 12 carrots in half
lengthways and place 4 halves on top of each tart, then
sprinkle over with coriander.

Garlic Mushroom & Peasto Tartlets

**MAKES 6 X 10CM LOOSE BOTTOMED
TART TINS
FREE FROM GLUTEN / DAIRY / NUTS**

*These simple tartlets are veritable flavour bombs. They
can be served cold or warmed through in the oven.*

Pastry
Vegetable oil, for brushing

140g brown rice flour, plus extra for dusting

75g cornflour

2 tsp sweet smoked paprika

60g vegetable margarine, chilled

2 eggs

Filling
1-2 tbsp rapeseed oil

3 cloves of garlic, finely chopped

250g mushrooms, thinly sliced

Topping
Batch of Peasto (see page 181)

2 tbsp pine nuts, toasted

Preheat the oven to 170°C / Gas 3.

Brush the tart tins with vegetable oil.

Weigh out all the dry ingredients for the pastry into a
food processor and add the margarine. Blitz until the mix
resembles breadcrumbs, this will take about 1 minute. From
time to time stop and make sure no dry mix is left in the
bottom. Add the eggs and continue to blitz. Mix until the
ingredients clump together. The mixture tends to stick to
the sides of the bowl, so you will need to scrape it out and
pop on to a liberally floured work surface.

With floured hands, mould the mixture into a ball of pastry.
Evenly divide the pastry into 6 portions, hand roll them into
balls and dust them with brown rice flour. Hand mould each
ball into a disc approximately 1-2cm thick. Press these discs
gently into the tart tins.

Space the tartlets out on a baking sheet. Bake for 18-20
minutes until the pastry feels firm and is light golden brown.
Once out of the oven, allow to cool completely before
turning out of their tins and adding the filling.

For the mushroom filling, heat 1 tablespoon of rapeseed
oil in a large frying pan on a medium heat. Add the garlic
and cook for 2-3 minutes, stirring every 30 seconds or so.
Once the garlic has softened, depending on the size of your
pan, add either all of the mushrooms or half at a time. The
mushrooms will reduce down in volume quite quickly once
you start to cook them, enabling you to fit more in the pan.
You may need to add another tablespoon of rapeseed oil at
this point if the pan has gone a bit dry. Fry the mushrooms
for 6-7 minutes, stirring fairly frequently. When ready they
will have started to turn a golden brown and will smell
amazing. Set to one side to cool.

To assemble the tartlets, spoon the Peasto evenly between
the tartlet cases and layer the mushrooms on top. Finish by
sprinkling with toasted pine nuts.

Once assembled best eaten
on the day

TIP

You can make the Peasto and pastry
cases ahead of time and freeze them

Me on the left in the first test
kitchen circa **1976** with beloved Mog

Rachel Rhodes and I in the
Guildford kitchen. Good times!

My high tech delivery system which
cost me a princely **£50** in 1998

Winchester Farmers Market
in **2000**

Toad In The Hole
with Red Onion & Rosemary

MAKES 1 TRAYBAKE
FREE FROM GLUTEN / DAIRY / NUTS

Like most of our savouries, we designed this to be a veritable vegetable fest. My memories of this dish feature big fat Lincolnshire sausages and Yorkshire pudding batter. Scrumptious in its own way, but not a vegetable to be seen. Our version includes a bonus layer of sweet potato plus greenery added to the batter. Our favourite gluten free veggie sausages are by The Somerset Sausage Company and they do mail order.

Batter

50g polenta

25g tapioca flour

25g sorghum flour

1½ tsp gluten free baking powder

125ml plant-based milk

100g dairy free spread

2 eggs

Base

1 large sweet potato, peeled and cut into slices approximately 1cm thick

1 medium sized red onion, cut into chunky slices

1 tbsp rapeseed oil, plus extra for brushing

½ tsp of cracked black pepper

Toads

6 vegetarian and gluten free sausages

Spinach layer

1 tsp rapeseed oil

2 garlic cloves, finely chopped

4 large handfuls of spinach leaves, washed and roughly chopped

¼ tsp of salt

¼ tsp of cracked black pepper

Finishing

1 sprig of fresh rosemary, finely snipped

Preheat the oven to 180°C / Gas 4.

Brush the traybake tin with rapeseed oil.

Mix the batter ingredients together in a bowl with an electric mixer on high speed for 1 minute until a smooth batter is formed. Put in the fridge to chill for 30 minutes whilst you cook the base and sausages.

Pop the base ingredients into a roasting tin, mix well with your hands and make sure the potato slices are spread out in the bottom of the tin, not piled up on top of each other. They will form the bottom layer of this dish. Roast for 20 minutes. The potatoes should be just starting to brown and caramelise.

Put the sausages into a separate roasting tin and pop in the oven at the same time as the base. Cook as per the instructions on the packet. Remove from the oven and set to one side until required.

Increase the oven to 200°C / Gas 6.

To make the spinach layer, warm the rapeseed oil in a frying pan on a high heat. Turn to a medium heat and add the garlic, spinach, salt and pepper and cook for approximately 1 minute, or until the spinach leaves just begin to wilt. Remove from the heat and set to one side.

Place the cooked sweet potato slices and onion in the bottom of the traybake tin to form the base. Once the spinach mixture has cooled slightly, spread it over the base, making sure it is evenly distributed. Pour the batter over the top, and place the sausages into the batter, pushed down slightly so they're partly submerged. Finally, sprinkle the rosemary over the top.

Bake for 30 minutes or until firm and light golden brown. Serve whilst piping hot.

Keeps in the fridge for 3 days. Can be frozen

You can use watercress and/or rocket as an alternative to the spinach in the batter

Hearty Veggie Hot Pot

MAKES 1 X 20CM CASSEROLE DISH
FREE FROM GLUTEN / DAIRY / NUTS
VEGAN

This is another hearty, standby supper solution. Can be served on its own or with a pile of mash to soak up the juices. Chop all the vegetables into bite size pieces. By cooking the sweet potato slices separately and adding them at the end, you can be sure of a crispy top with no sogginess.

Hot Pot

2 onions, chopped

4 cloves garlic, chopped

2 tbsp fresh thyme, chopped

2 red peppers, deseeded and chopped

1 butternut squash, peeled and chopped

1 fennel bulb, chopped

2 tsp cracked black pepper

Olive oil, for drizzling

3 sprigs of fresh rosemary

2 bay leaves

2 tbsp liquid sweetener of choice

100g Arborio risotto rice

400ml gluten free and vegan vegetable stock

500g passata

Topping

1 large sweet potato, peeled and thinly sliced

Olive oil, for drizzling

1 tbsp fresh thyme, chopped

1 tbsp polenta

Preheat the oven to 200°C / Gas 6.

Line a baking sheet with baking parchment.

Place the onions, garlic, thyme, peppers, butternut squash, fennel and cracked black pepper into a roasting tin, and drizzle with olive oil. Mix everything together with a wooden spoon and roast for 15 minutes.

Reduce the oven to 180°C / Gas 4.

Tip the roasted vegetables into the casserole dish and add the rest of the hot pot ingredients. With a lid on, bake for approximately 45 minutes or until the mixture has thickened and the rice is cooked.

For the topping, place the sweet potato slices onto the lined baking sheet and drizzle with olive oil, thyme and polenta. Cook for 20-25 minutes along with the casserole, until they have started to crisp up. Aim to have these ready at the same time as the hot pot.

Once the hot pot is out of the oven, overlap the hot sweet potato slices on top and serve.

Keeps in the fridge
for 4 days

Dried lentils work really well
instead of the Arborio rice

SMASHING
SIDES

Veggies, coleslaw, salads & greens

Eat the rainbow is what they say, from red to purple every day

Chargrilled Broccoli with Chilli & Toasted Sesame Seeds

SERVES 4
FREE FROM GLUTEN / DAIRY / NUTS
VEGAN

This is such a lovely dressing, it takes seconds to whizz up and works well alongside other stir fried veggies such as asparagus, spring greens or baby leeks. We make a big bowl of rice noodles for the middle of the table then surround it with a selection of sides, together with a jug of dressing. People can then tailor make their own dish.

Broccoli

400g purple sprouting broccoli

Dressing

1 red chilli, finely chopped

2 garlic cloves, finely chopped

3-4 tbsp toasted sesame seed oil, plus extra for brushing

2 tbsp gluten free soy sauce

1 tbsp fresh ginger, finely chopped

1 tbsp fresh coriander, chopped

2 tbsp sesame seeds, toasted

Finishing

1 tbsp sesame seeds, toasted

Bring a pan of water to the boil. Prepare the broccoli by trimming off any woody stems. Place it into the boiling water and bring back to the boil for 1 minute. Strain and place into cold water to prevent it from cooking any further.

Place the dressing ingredients into a bowl and stir to combine. Set to one side.

Brush a griddle pan with toasted sesame seed oil and place on a high heat. Place the broccoli in the hot pan and press it down using a wooden spoon so that you get the lovely lines from the pan onto the broccoli, this will take 3-4 minutes. Place the broccoli in a serving bowl and pour the dressing on. Mix gently with a wooden spoon to ensure the dressing coats the broccoli. Sprinkle with the remaining toasted sesame seeds and serve.

Keeps in the fridge for 2 days

TIP

You can add coriander seeds too. You just need to dry roast them in a hot pan for 4-5 minutes and crush them with a spoon

Celeriac, Sage & Hazelnut Bake

MAKES 1 X 23CM FLAN DISH
FREE FROM GLUTEN

This wows everyone who tries it. Delicious partnered with crispy jacket potatoes and simple salad. It tastes sophisticated but it truly is a "bish bash bosh" type of dish. The only thing to take care with is slicing the celeriac as thinly as you can.

Butter, for greasing
1 medium celeriac, peeled, halved and thinly sliced
300ml whipping cream or single cream
14 fresh sage leaves
½ tsp ground white pepper
75g hazelnuts, toasted and roughly chopped

Preheat the oven to 180°C / Gas 4.

Lightly butter the flan dish.

Layer half the celeriac in the flan dish. Add splashes of cream, sage, pepper and toasted hazelnuts before layering up with more celeriac.

Cover with the rest of the cream, sage, pepper and toasted hazelnuts. Bake for 30 minutes.

Serve warm.

Keeps in the fridge for 2 days. Add cream or milk to loosen it up a bit

TIP
Wild mushrooms can be added or used instead of the celeriac if preferred

Butternut Squash with Coriander & Toasted Seeds

SERVES 4-6
FREE FROM GLUTEN / DAIRY / NUTS
VEGAN

This is so easy to do and works really well served warm or cold. We serve it alongside the Gnocchi, Cheese & Tomato Bake (see page 91).

1 medium butternut squash, peeled, deseeded and cut into bite size pieces
2 tbsp rapeseed oil, plus extra for drizzling
½ tsp cracked black pepper
1 tbsp coriander seeds
2 tbsp sunflower seeds
3 tbsp fresh coriander, chopped, plus extra for sprinkling
1 tbsp liquid sweetener of choice

Preheat the oven to 180°C / Gas 4.

Place the prepared butternut squash in a roasting tin, and drizzle with a little rapeseed oil and sprinkle with pepper. Roast for 30-35 minutes until the squash is just starting to caramelise around the edges.

Place the coriander seeds in a pan on a high heat for 2-3 minutes and crush them with the back of a spoon. Add the sunflower seeds and toast for another 2 minutes until they start to slightly brown. They'll also start to smell wonderful.

In a bowl, toss the roasted butternut squash with the toasted seeds and coriander. Using a fork, mix the oil and liquid sweetener in a measuring jug to make a dressing. Add to the butternut squash and stir with a wooden spoon, ensuring the squash is coated.

To finish, sprinkle with coriander.

Keeps in the fridge for 3 days

TIP
Chantenay carrots roasted whole work just as well as the squash. Similarly, the coriander can be swapped for sage if you prefer

How to make your squash bird feeder

tweet tweet

1. Cut a butternut squash or pumpkin in half and scoop out the insides leaving a thick wall

2. Place two sticks through the middle of the squash for the birds to perch on

3. Fill the hole with seeds, dried fruit and *yummy* berries

4. Tie pieces of rope onto the sticks to hang onto a tree

Please feed the birds!

Super Easy Roasted Vegetables

SERVES 4-6
FREE FROM GLUTEN / DAIRY
VEGAN

We tend not to peel our root veg and give them a good scrub instead. We've listed redcurrant jelly in the ingredients as it's easily available and works well. If you can get hold of artisan or home made fruit jelly to use instead, all the better.

Roast vegetables

3 red onions, cut into wedges

2 parsnips, washed and cut into chunky chips

3 carrots, washed and cut into thick slices

1 head of celeriac, peeled and cut into chunky chips

2 lemons, cut into quarters

¼ tsp salt

¼ tsp cracked black pepper

Dressing

5 tbsp rapeseed oil

2 tbsp liquid sweetener of choice

2 tsp dried thyme

2½ tbsp redcurrant jelly

Topping

3 sprigs of fresh rosemary

20g flaked almonds

Preheat the oven to 200°C / Gas 6.

Place your prepared vegetables into a roasting tin and add the lemons, sprinkle with the salt and pepper to taste, and mix with your hands.

To make the dressing, mix the rapeseed oil, liquid sweetener, thyme and jelly in a bowl using a whisk.

Pour the dressing over the vegetables. Poke the rosemary sprigs down into the vegetables so the flavour releases as it cooks.

Pop in the oven for 30-35 minutes until the veggies are just starting to caramelise around the edges. During the last 5 minutes of cooking time sprinkle the flaked almonds over the top to toast them.

Serve warm or cold.

Keeps in the fridge for 3 days

TIP
For the finest jellies and jams take a look at thymeaftertime.co.uk

Sweet Potato Champ with Chard

SERVES 4-6
FREE FROM GLUTEN / NUTS

This will have Champ purists all a flutter as we've strayed from the traditional, straight potato version. The water content of sweet potatoes does vary so you may need to add a little more milk a drop at a time to get the right creamy consistency of mashed potato. Best served hot with an additional knob of butter on top.

750g sweet potatoes, peeled and chopped

100g chard

1 bunch spring onions, chopped

110ml milk

50g butter

¼ tsp salt

¼ tsp ground white pepper

Finishing

1 tbsp fresh parsley, chopped

Boil the sweet potatoes for 15 minutes or until cooked through. Drain and set aside for a couple of minutes to dry off. Then either mash them or put through a ricer.

Prepare the chard by placing it into a large bowl of cold water to wash then pull the stems from the leaves and keep separately. Roughly chop the leaves and place them with the spring onions and milk in a plastic bowl. Microwave for 3 minutes on high power.

Chop the chard stems into 1cm lengths. Melt the butter in a frying pan and add the chard stems. Gently fry until the stems are softened but still slightly crunchy. Add the salt, pepper, the cooked chard leaves, milk, spring onions and any remaining butter from the pan to the mashed sweet potato and mix well. The mash needs to hold its shape. You may need to add a little milk if the mash is too stiff.

Finally, top with chopped parsley and serve whilst piping hot.

Keeps in the fridge for 2 days

TIP

Spinach can be swapped for the chard if you prefer. You can just pop the whole spinach leaves into the milk and onion mixture and heat for 1 minute in the microwave

Chickpea, Chilli & Olive Salad

SERVES 4
FREE FROM GLUTEN / DAIRY / NUTS
VEGAN

This recipe came about by actually being inspired by something I ate at a late night petrol station. Doing the mileage out on the road selling Honeybuns, I'm often in search of a nutritious snack. I tried one of these little pots of salad with a Greek exporter's label on and was blown away. It's so simple and really rather lovely.

1 tbsp olive oil

1 red pepper, finely chopped

1 small red onion, finely chopped

½ - 1 fresh red chilli, finely chopped
(depending on your appetite for heat)

70g black olives, pitted and roughly chopped

1 tsp sumac or zest of 1 lemon

400g tinned chickpeas, rinsed and drained

2 tbsp fresh oregano, chopped

Finishing

1 tbsp fresh oregano, chopped

Warm the oil in a frying pan on a high heat and add the pepper, onion and chilli. Stir from time to time and cook for 5-6 minutes until the pepper and onion has started to soften. Turn down to a medium heat and add the olives, sumac or lemon zest and chickpeas and cook for a further 2 minutes. Remove from the heat and stir in the fresh oregano, which will wilt slightly. Transfer to a serving bowl. Allow to cool before sprinkling with more oregano.

Keeps in the fridge for 2 days

TIP
You can also add crumbled feta if you want to push the boat out a little, bearing in mind this would make the recipe non-vegan

Cucumber, Feta & Lemon Salad

SERVES 4
FREE FROM GLUTEN / NUTS

This is a ridiculously easy salad to assemble and tastes really fresh and clean. We serve it on a flat tray together with the Chickpea, Chilli & Olive Salad and Sprouting Super Salad, both also featured in this chapter. Our very talented food stylist, Bianca, cut the cucumber lengthways and deseeded it by scooping the seeds out with a spoon. This was for the purposes of the photo, but feel free to roughly chop it as it doesn't affect the taste.

1 cucumber, chopped

Juice and zest of ½ a lemon

½ tsp cracked black pepper

12 mint leaves, chopped, plus whole leaves for sprinkling

100g vegetarian feta, crumbled

1 tsp pink peppercorns, partly crushed

¼ tsp sea salt flakes

Avocado or olive oil, generously drizzled

Place the cucumber into a large bowl and squeeze the lemon juice over. Add the pepper and chopped mint and gently mix together with your hands or a wooden spoon. Crumble the feta over the top and add the lemon zest. Finish off with the crushed pink peppercorns, whole mint leaves, salt and drizzle with avocado or olive oil.

 Best eaten on the day

 TIP Melon works very well instead of, or as well as, the cucumber

CUCUMBER RAINBOWS

how
nice

Polenta Roasties with Wholegrain Mustard

SERVES 4
FREE FROM GLUTEN / DAIRY / NUTS
VEGAN

Our favourite potato for roasting is the King Edward, as you can get fluffiness without them falling apart. Maris Piper and Desiree also yield good results.

150ml rapeseed oil, plus extra for brushing

8 medium potatoes

35g polenta

4 tbsp gluten free wholegrain mustard

½ tbsp cracked black pepper

Preheat the oven to 200°C / Gas 6.

Brush a roasting tin with rapeseed oil.

Bring a pan of water to the boil. Peel and cut the potatoes into wedges. Add the potatoes to the pan and boil for 20 minutes. You want the potatoes to retain their shape but if you gently applied pressure with a fork they'd fall apart.

Drain the potatoes in a colander and shake them around to fluff them up. Place the potatoes in a bowl, add the polenta and shake again. You want to roughen up the surfaces of the potatoes but you don't want to be so vigorous that they totally fall apart either. Pop any bits of potato and polenta that collected in the bowl into the roasting tin as they will crisp up.

Using a fork, mix the oil, mustard and pepper together in a measuring jug.

Pop the potatoes in the roasting tin, then pour the oil, mustard and pepper mixture over the top. Using a large metal spoon, tumble the potatoes gently to ensure they are thoroughly coated in the mixture.

Pop the potatoes into the oven for 45-50 minutes. They should go crispy and dark brown around edges. Serve piping hot.

Keeps in the fridge for up to 2 days

TIP

Try adding freshly snipped rosemary or thyme over the potatoes for added flavour

Rat-A-Tat-Touille

SERVES 4-6
FREE FROM GLUTEN / DAIRY / NUTS
VEGAN

This is a movable feast as we lob pretty much any seasonal vegetables in! Delicious served as a main with a chunky slice of our Seeded Loaf to mop up the juices (see page 51). When we say roughly chopped, we mean bite sized pieces.

1 red onion, peeled and roughly chopped

100g cherry tomatoes, halved

1 small courgette, cut into 1cm discs

1 red pepper, roughly chopped

4 garlic cloves, finely chopped

70g olives, pitted and halved

2 tbsp olive oil

1 tbsp gluten free balsamic vinegar

¼ tsp fennel seeds

1 tbsp fresh oregano, chopped

1 tbsp fresh tarragon, chopped

400g tinned cherry tomatoes with the juice

3 tbsp vegan red wine

Preheat the oven to 200°C / Gas 6.

Place all of the vegetables, garlic and olives in a roasting tin. Add the olive oil, balsamic vinegar, fennel seeds, oregano and tarragon. Tumble the mixture together, either using your hands or a wooden spoon. The aim is to mix the vegetables up and coat them with the oil and herbs. Place in the oven for 20 minutes.

The vegetables will have just started to char around the edges. Add the tinned tomatoes and red wine. Stir and return to the oven for another 10 minutes.

Serve warm or cold.

Keeps in the fridge for 3 days

TIP

Olives can be swapped for capers if you prefer. Button mushrooms, aubergine and butternut squash also work well in this recipe

Companion Plums

MAKES A 500ML KILNER JAR'S WORTH
FREE FROM GLUTEN / DAIRY / NUTS

1/8 tsp cinnamon

1/4 tsp ground star anise

12 large plums

4 tbsp runny honey

So called, as they can accompany a whole range of dishes from a Ploughman's to a veggie roast. If you're not keen on the aniseed flavour of star anise, you can substitute ground mixed spice. The plums can be served warm or cold.

De-stone and dice the plums into approximately 1cm cubes. Place in a saucepan with the honey, ground star anise and cinnamon.

Place the pan on a medium heat for 12-14 minutes. Stir every couple of minutes with a wooden spoon to prevent the mixture from sticking.

The sauce is ready when the fruit has started to break down. You will end up with a mixture of small chunks and some fruity sauce.

Remove from the heat and allow to cool completely before decanting into a sterilised jar.

Keeps in the fridge for 2 weeks

TIP
Fab served with cheese and is also delicious with dessert and ice cream

Sprouting Super Salad with Lemony Croutons

FREE FROM GLUTEN
DAIRY FREE & VEGAN WITHOUT LEMONY CROUTONS

This is a hearty salad, packed with nourishing goodies. You can either sprout your own seeds or you can buy packs of ready sprouted mixes in the chilled section of some supermarkets. It's important to thoroughly rinse them with cold water before using. You can heat them through in a wok for 3-4 minutes with a little oil if you prefer not to eat them raw. We prefer them raw though.

Salad

200g Chantenay carrots

2 tbsp maple syrup

1 tbsp avocado or olive oil

200g sprouting seed mix, washed and rinsed

70g skin on whole hazelnuts, toasted

2 tbsp fresh flat leaf parsley or coriander, chopped

Dressing

Finely grated zest and juice of 1 small orange

1 tbsp avocado or olive oil

2 tsp maple syrup

2 tsp cracked black pepper

1 tbsp gluten free balsamic vinegar

1 garlic clove, crushed

Finish

1-2 tbsp fresh flat leaf parsley or coriander, finely chopped

Batch of Lemony Croutons (see page 188)

Preheat the oven to 200°C / Gas 6.

Wash and top the carrots, leaving any small carrots whole and if there are bigger ones you can always slice in half lengthways to help even out cooking times.

Pop the carrots in a roasting tin and drizzle with maple syrup and avocado or olive oil. Roast for 18-20 minutes, until they are soft when pierced with a fork. After roasting, shake the tin to make sure the juices coat the carrots.

Allow to cool. We like this salad served whilst the carrots are still slightly warm.

Place the sprouting seeds into a bowl and mix with the toasted hazelnuts, carrots and chopped parsley or coriander.

For the dressing, mix the orange zest and juice, avocado or olive oil and maple syrup. Add the cracked black pepper, balsamic vinegar and garlic. Add the dressing to the salad and toss to coat.

Sprinkle over with chopped herbs and Lemony Croutons to finish.

Best eaten on the day

TIP

Runny honey can be used instead of maple syrup (but then it won't be vegan!)

Dunc's Slaw

SERVES 6
FREE FROM GLUTEN / NUTS
DAIRY FREE & VEGAN IF USING
DRESSING NO 2

So called after the coleslaw my brother Duncan serves at his Newcastle eatery, Coop. Both the dressings work well, and please see the introduction for suggested dairy free cream cheeses. For the photo we created "lunch jars" by simply placing the dressing at the bottom of the jar and layering up with the coleslaw ingredients. The idea being you can stir up the layers just before you tuck in.

Coleslaw

1 apple, grated
1 fennel bulb, cored and thinly sliced
1 carrot, grated
¼ red cabbage, thinly sliced
25g pine nuts, toasted
½ tbsp fennel seeds, toasted
100g radishes, thinly sliced
2 tbsp fresh parsley, chopped
½ tsp ground white pepper

Dressing no 1

200g crème fraiche
Juice of 1 lemon
2 tbsp gluten free Dijon mustard

Dressing no 2 (dairy free and vegan)

2 ripe avocados, peeled and stoned
Juice of 1 lemon
200g dairy free and vegan garlic and herb cream cheese

Place all the coleslaw ingredients into a large mixing bowl and gently stir with a wooden spoon until they are mixed up.

For dressing no 1, stir the ingredients together in a bowl. Combine with the coleslaw and serve. It's a pourable dressing.

For dressing no 2, either mash the ingredients together with a fork or use a food processor and blitz until smooth. Combine with the coleslaw and serve. This dressing has more of a creamy, paste like texture.

Keeps for 3 days
in the fridge

TIP

If making this in the winter, the radishes
can be swapped with sliced sprouts

Waldorfey Salad

SERVES 4
FREE FROM GLUTEN

This is our pimped up take on the classic. The ginger works particularly well with the blue cheese. You could also try serving it with the Companion Plums (see page 127) before you tuck in.

5 pears, Conference or Comice

20g stem ginger in syrup, finely chopped

Pinch of cinnamon

1-2 tsp caraway seeds, to taste

70g walnut halves, toasted

20g pine nuts, toasted

1 bag or bunch of watercress leaves, washed

100g Dorset Blue Vinny or Cambozola

Avocado or olive oil

Preheat the oven to 200°C / Gas 6.

Cut each pear in half, core and de stalk (peel if preferred), and slice into wedges. Place them on a baking sheet and drizzle with a little of the ginger syrup from the jar of stem ginger. Sprinkle the pears with the cinnamon and the caraway seeds. Pop in the oven for 20-25 minutes. When they are ready, they'll go a little brown around the edges and a skewer will go easily into the flesh.

Allow the pears to cool slightly, and place into a mixing bowl. Add the ginger, walnuts and pine nuts and shake around to combine. Add the watercress and lightly mix by hand or with a wooden spoon, taking care to keep the pear slices intact.

Tip the salad onto a large flat platter and then crumble the Dorset Blue Vinny or Cambozola over. Drizzle with the avocado or olive oil and serve.

Best eaten straight away

Nectarines or peaches could be used instead of pears

PERFECT

PUDDINGS

Cheesecakes, tarts & truffles

THERE ARE DAYS WHEN WE JUST DON'T HAVE TIME TO MAKE A PUDDING FROM SCRATCH, SO WHY NOT SERVE UP ONE OF OUR READY MADE GLUTEN FREE CAKES INSTEAD? THEY TASTE DELICIOUS WITH ICE CREAM OR CUSTARD

A PERFECT PUD
FOR SH♥RING

Chocolate & Raspberry Pizza

MAKES 1 X LARGE PIZZA
FREE FROM GLUTEN

This is a lovely pudding to share. Try serving it on a wooden board and scatter the topping loosely over the pizza base, keeping everything looking slightly undone and rustic.

Pizza base

1 egg

85g Date Paste (see page 197)

150g ground hazelnuts

1½ tsp gluten free baking powder

125g butter

½ tsp vanilla paste

100g gluten free oats

2 tbsp gluten free cocoa powder

75g milk chocolate, chunks or buttons

75g white chocolate, chunks or buttons

75g dark chocolate, chunks or buttons

Avocado ganache

½ ripe avocado, mashed

100g dark chocolate, melted

1 tbsp honey

Raspberry topping

200g raspberries, fresh or frozen and defrosted

250g mascarpone

40g white chocolate, melted

40g milk chocolate, melted

Preheat the oven to 170°C / Gas 3.

Place all of the base ingredients, except the 3 chocolate varieties, into a mixing bowl and beat with an electric mixer on high speed for 1 minute. Once the ingredients are combined, add the chocolate and stir in by hand.

Place the mixture between two sheets of parchment and roll to a 25-30cm circle. Remove the top sheet of paper and transfer the bottom sheet with the pizza base onto a baking sheet. Bake in the oven for 12 minutes or until firm to the touch. Set to one side and allow to cool.

To make the avocado ganache, place the avocado, chocolate and honey into a bowl and mix with an electric mixer on high speed for 1 minute until a smooth paste is formed. Whilst the ganache is still warm, spread it over the cooled pizza base using a palette knife, leaving 2cm from the sides.

Crush 150g of the raspberries with the back of a fork. Place spoonfuls of the crushed raspberries and mascarpone in little piles over the pizza. Finally, drizzle with the melted chocolates and sprinkle with the remaining whole raspberries.

Keeps in the fridge for 2 days. The base can be pre baked and frozen

If you have fresh mint leaves to hand these look good scattered over the top

Lemon Love Pudding

SERVES 2
FREE FROM GLUTEN

These lovely little puddings are a bit of a hybrid. Think lemon meringue pie meets Eton Mess. Super swift to make, and they taste sensational. You'll need two pretty glass dessert dishes which you can pick up for next to nothing in charity shops and car boots.

2 generous slices of St Clements Cake (see page 69)

Generous glug of Limoncello

4 generous tbsp gluten free lemon curd

12 segments of tinned mandarin, clementine or satsuma

6-8 tbsp Greek yoghurt

2 tbsp meringue (you can use shop bought small nests or make your own)

Finely grated zest of 2 lemons

Cut each St Clements Cake slice in half lengthways and then into 4 squares or heart shapes with a cookie cutter.

Pop them into a shallow bowl and pour a generous glug of Limoncello over them. Allow this to soak in for a couple of minutes.

Spread half of the lemon curd over the Limoncello soaked cake pieces and transfer them into your 2 glass serving dishes. The idea is for the cake pieces to line the outside of each dish, with the lemon curd facing inwards. You can use spare bits of cake to put in the bottom of the dish to stop the side cake bits falling down. Add the fruit segments.

In a separate bowl, mix the Greek yoghurt with the remaining lemon curd and spoon into the dishes. Crumble the meringue pieces over the top and decorate with lemon zest. Chill for 1 hour or more before sharing... if you can bear to!

Keeps in the fridge for 2 days

TIP

Using the similar layering idea you could try a dark chocolate brownie black forest gateaux using cherries, kirsch and brownies

5

A glass full of love
(and cake)

Coppice Cream Tea

SERVES 4-6
FREE FROM GLUTEN / DAIRY

We've named this beautiful pudding Coppice in celebration of the hedgerow goodies that are showcased in this dish; namely the blackberries and hazelnuts. The texture of the base is a blend of meringue and sponge. For extra ooh la la try adding a blackberry liqueur or Somerset Cider Brandy.

Filling

200ml orange juice

75g runny honey

300g fresh or frozen blackberries

1 tbsp cornflour mixed to a thin paste with approximately 2 tbsp cold water

Base

3 egg whites

½ tsp vanilla paste

200g Date Paste (see page 197)

75g ground hazelnuts

40g hazelnuts, roughly chopped and toasted

Coconut cream

160ml coconut cream

1 tsp vanilla paste

Topping

35g hazelnuts, roughly chopped and toasted

 Best eaten on the day. Base can be frozen

 TIP The base also works really well with 100g of runny honey instead of the 200g of Date Paste

Preheat the oven to 170°C / Gas 3.

Line a baking sheet with baking parchment. Place a metal bowl in the freezer.

Place the orange juice and honey with 150g of the blackberries in a saucepan. Bring to the boil and then lower to a medium heat and simmer gently for 3-4 minutes. Remove the mixture from the heat and allow to cool slightly before sieving it. To do this, press the blackberries firmly through the sieve with the back of a spoon, collecting the strained juice in a bowl. Discard any remnants left in the sieve.

Place the juice back in the pan, bring to the boil, then remove from the heat before adding the cornflour paste. Whisk immediately to prevent lumps from forming. Once thickened, take off the heat and pour into a clean container, suitable to chill in the fridge. When cooled add the remaining blackberries and chill until required.

To make the base, whisk the egg whites with an electric whisk on high speed for approximately 3 minutes to form stiff peaks. In a new bowl, add the vanilla paste to the date paste and mix using an electric mixer on high speed for 1 minute, until the pastes have combined. Add a small amount of the whisked egg whites at a time to the paste mixture, and fold in using a metal spoon until all of the egg whites are combined. Add the ground and toasted hazelnuts to the mixture and mix in with a spoon, taking care not to over beat and lose the fluffiness of the whisked egg whites. Spread the mixture into a 23cm circle on the lined baking sheet. Gently create a hollow in the middle leaving the sides slightly deeper, like a Pavlova.

Bake for 20 minutes. Remove from the oven and set aside to cool. Do not attempt to remove the base from the baking parchment until it has cooled completely. Place the base on a serving plate or board.

Whilst the base is cooking, retrieve the metal bowl from the freezer and add the coconut cream and vanilla paste. Whisk with an electric mixer on high speed for 1-2 minutes, or until you have a whipped cream consistency. Spoon the coconut cream into the hollow of the cooled base, then spoon the blackberry mixture over the top of this. To finish, sprinkle the toasted hazelnuts on top. Serve immediately.

Low Rise Rhubarb & Ginger Cheesecake

MAKES 1 X 23CM LOOSE BOTTOMED CAKE TIN
FREE FROM GLUTEN / NUTS

This is a no fuss pudding, which looks humble and low profile yet tastes sensational. The base layer tastes like homemade digestives shot through with ginger. Roasting the rhubarb takes the edge off its tartness although if you want to skip this stage you can add more honey to the cream cheese layer instead.

Rhubarb layer

300g rhubarb

2 tbsp runny honey

½ a batch of rhubarb Half Jam (see page 197)

250g tub vegetarian cream cheese

300ml double cream

40g stem ginger in syrup or glacé ginger, finely chopped

Base

125g Date Paste (see page 197)

125g milled flaxseed, sunflower and pumpkin seed blend

140g polenta

150g butter, melted

40g pumpkin seeds, toasted and chopped

40g stem ginger in syrup or glacé ginger, finely chopped

2 tsp ground ginger

Preheat the oven to 180°C / Gas 4.

Line the base of the cake tin with baking parchment.

Top and tail the rhubarb, and cut into chunks. Place in a roasting tin, drizzle with honey, and roast for 15 minutes. Set aside to cool.

To make the base, place all of the ingredients into a bowl and beat with an electric mixer on high speed for 1 minute until they are well combined. Press this mixture firmly into the bottom of the cake tin using the back of a metal spoon. Bake in the oven for 15 minutes or until lightly golden. Leave to cool completely before removing the base from the tin. Spread the rhubarb half jam over the top of the base using a palette knife.

To make the rhubarb layer, place 250g of the roasted rhubarb and any roasting juice from the tin into a mixing bowl, setting aside the remaining rhubarb for later. Add the cream cheese, double cream and ginger and beat with an electric mixer on high speed. This will take 3-4 minutes for the mixture to thicken up; you need a spreadable consistency. Using a palette knife, spread the mixture over the cooled and jammed base and top with your reserved roast rhubarb. You can then chill the cheesecake until you are ready to demolish it.

Keeps in the fridge for 3 days. Base can be frozen

TIP

Make an extra base, bake then break into bits, toast and sprinkle over the top of the pudding

High Summer Slices

MAKES 6 SLICES
FREE FROM GLUTEN / NUTS
DAIRY FREE IF USING FILLING NO 2

The base recipe is really versatile and works well as a sweet pizza base, it can also be rolled, once baked, to make a roulade style pudding. We've included a traditional dairy cream filling as well as a dairy free filling giving you the choice. The cream filling can be spread or piped and any summer fruits can be used.

Base

200g Prune Paste (see page 197)

2 eggs

115g dairy free cream cheese

115g milled flaxseed, sunflower and pumpkin seed blend

2 tbsp gluten and dairy free cocoa powder

1 tsp vanilla paste

3 tbsp runny honey

Strawberries

400g fresh strawberries, hulled

1tsp cracked black pepper

1 tbsp fresh mint, chopped, plus extra leaves for finishing

1 tsp gluten free balsamic vinegar

1-2 tbsp runny honey

Filling no 1

150ml double cream

250g mascarpone

2 tbsp runny honey

Filling no 2 (dairy free)

2 batches of Coconut Milk Ice (see page 198)

Keeps in the fridge
for 1 day

TIP

The base can be made ahead
of time and frozen

We love summer

And we love these slices

Preheat the oven to 180°C / Gas 4.

Line a baking sheet with baking parchment.

Mix all the base ingredients in a large bowl using an electric mixer on high speed for 1 minute until the ingredients have combined. Using a palette knife spread the mixture into a 28cm x 26cm rectangle on the baking sheet. Bake in the oven for 14-16 minutes or until set. Lift the baking parchment with the baked base onto a wire rack to cool.

While the base is cooling, thinly slice the strawberries and place into a large bowl. Add the pepper, mint, vinegar and honey and gently stir to combine the ingredients. Place in the fridge.

If using filling no 1, whip the double cream lightly until it just starts to thicken. Add the mascarpone and honey and continue beating until the mixture holds its own shape.

To assemble the pudding, cut your base lengthways into 3 equal rectangles and trim them to tidy up. Cut each of the 3 rectangles into 6 even sized rectangles, leaving you with 18 mini rectangles.

Place 6 of the rectangles on a plate or a board to form the base. Spread half the cream mixture onto the bases using a palette knife to make it smooth. If using filling no 2 simply scoop onto the base.

Next, spoon a third of the strawberries over the filling. Place the next 6 rectangles on top of the strawberry and cream filling layer and repeat the process by using the rest of the filling and another third of the strawberries.

Finish by placing your final 6 rectangles on top and spoon the remaining strawberries and juice liberally over the assembled slices. If you are not serving this straight away, then we recommend finishing the top layer of strawberries at the last minute so the strawberries don't fall off. Decorate with mint leaves.

Appleberry Charlotte

MAKES 1 x 18CM PUDDING BOWL
FREE FROM GLUTEN

Although this pudding looks formidable, if you can cobble a trifle together you will be able to make it with ease. Either shop bought or homemade custard works well here. The sponge casing can be made ahead of time and frozen until required.

Sponge casing

175g butter, melted, plus extra for brushing

2 eggs

140g crystallised sweetener of choice

70g ground almonds

70g sorghum flour

25g ground golden flaxseed

1½ tsp gluten free baking powder

1 tsp vanilla paste

Filling

1 large cooking apple, peeled, cored and chopped

75g runny honey

75g raspberries

300ml gluten free custard

Finishing

2 tbsp runny honey, to glaze

Best eaten
on the day

TIP

You can use alternative fruits, including
blackcurrants, blackberries, cherries and quince

Preheat the oven to 170°C / Gas 3.

Line a 450g loaf tin with baking parchment and brush with melted butter. Line the bottom of the pudding bowl with a disc of baking parchment and brush the sides liberally with melted butter.

Place the eggs into a large bowl followed by the dry ingredients for the sponge casing. Then add the melted butter and vanilla paste and mix with an electric mixer on high speed for approximately 1 minute, until the ingredients are combined. Pour the mixture into the loaf tin and bake for 35-40 minutes or until firm to the touch. Allow to cool for 10 minutes before lifting the loaf out of the tin onto a wire rack to cool completely.

Next, place the apple in a pan with the honey and cook for 10 minutes until the apple is at the point of collapse. Set to one side.

To assemble the Charlotte, cut your sponge loaf into 1cm thick slices. Reserve a fifth of the loaf, which will be used to create a lid. Completely line the pudding bowl with the remaining sponge slices, hand squidging the slices into position to ensure there are no gaps. Pour the custard into the empty Charlotte, then add the apples and raspberries. Using your reserved sponge slices, create a lid to enclose the filling. Again you need to ensure there are no gaps, as this will form the base of your pudding once you invert it. Place the bowl on a baking sheet and bake for 30 minutes. The pudding will look toasted on top and slightly crispy.

Leave to sit for 30 minutes before serving so that it is just warm. This also makes it more stable and easier to remove from the bowl. To remove from the bowl, place a plate over the top of the pudding bowl and invert the pudding onto the plate.

To glaze the pudding, heat the runny honey either in a pan or the microwave. With a pastry brush, liberally brush the Charlotte with honey all over the top and the sides. Devour with relish.

Don't use insecticides
and pesticides

Choose a variety of plants to
attract a variety of wildlife

Choose sunny and sheltered
spots to plant the flowers

Well watered plants will produce far
more nectar for hungry bees and butterflies

For bee friendly plant inspo take a look at
rosybee.com

Buddleia

Lupin

Verbena bonariensis

Bee balm

Sunflower

Marjoram

Thistle

Black-eyed Susan

Borage

Lavender

Crocus

Calendula

Almond, Chocolate & Cherry Truffles

MAKES 24 TRUFFLES
FREE FROM GLUTEN / DAIRY
VEGAN

These little scamps are incredibly easy to make and you can use either shop bought boozy whole cherries or make your own. To do this, simply store fresh cherries in a Kilner jar with a brandy of your choice. We love Somerset Cider Brandy, and this artisan producer also sells cherries in Somerset Apple Eau de Vie online at ciderbrandy.co.uk. You will need to warn guests that the cherries contain stones. You can always pit the cherries beforehand, the downside to this is that they tend to go soggy without the stones in.

100g Prune Paste (see page 197)

125g ground almonds

25g rapeseed oil

25g gluten free, dairy free and vegan cocoa powder

4 tsp liquid sweetener of choice

25g coconut flakes, toasted

55g nibbed almonds, toasted

4 tsp of the alcohol the cherries are stored in

24 brandied whole cherries, either homemade or shop bought

150g dairy free and vegan dark chocolate

Add all the ingredients, apart from the whole cherries and the chocolate, into the food processor and blitz until a dough is formed. This will take up to 1 minute, and when squeezed in your hand, the dough will hold together.

Evenly divide the dough into 24 and hand roll into balls. Indent the centre of each ball with your thumb, then pop a cherry into the indentation and wrap the dough around to fully enclose the cherry. Roll each ball in the palm of your hand to make a smooth, round truffle.

Place the chocolate in a microwaveable bowl and melt in the microwave for 30 second bursts on medium power until the chocolate has melted. Be careful not to overheat the chocolate as it will burn. If the chocolate has nearly melted but still has few lumps remaining, it is safer to remove from the microwave and stir these lumps in to melt them. Allow the chocolate to cool slightly, then roll each truffle in the chocolate, and place them on a sheet of baking parchment to set. These are ready to eat as soon as the chocolate has set.

Keeps in the fridge
for 7 days.
Can be frozen

For a nut free version, substitute the ground almonds for a milled flaxseed, sunflower and pumpkin seed blend, and swap the almonds for either chopped pumpkin or sunflower seeds

Chocolate, Prune & Avocado Tart

**MAKES 1 X 20CM LOOSE BOTTOMED
CAKE TIN
FREE FROM GLUTEN / DAIRY
VEGAN**

*This looks and tastes sophisticated but is in fact a doddle
to make. The crust mixture doesn't need to be rolled,
just hand pressed into the tin. No technical pastry skills
required. We like the intensity of the dark chocolate
topping, but if you have a sweeter tooth, feel free to up
the ante.*

Crust

50g unrefined coconut oil, plus extra for brushing

200g ground hazelnuts

40g maple syrup

Topping

300g dairy free and vegan dark chocolate

1 ripe avocado, mashed to a pulp

2 tbsp vegan Armagnac or other brandy

2 tsp instant espresso coffee granules, dissolved
in a little hot water

25 stoned prunes (nice plump ones)

50g hazelnuts, roughly chopped and toasted

Preheat the oven to 150°C / Gas 4.

Line the bottom of the cake tin with baking parchment, and
brush the sides with coconut oil.

To make the crust, place the coconut oil in a food processor
with the ground hazelnuts and maple syrup. Blitz until well
mixed, wet and crumbly. Spoon the mixture into the tin and
press it to cover the base and sides. You can use your hands
to make sure that it is firmly pressed and evenly spread.
Bake for 12-15 minutes. Set aside and allow to cool.

Place 200g of the chocolate in a microwaveable bowl and
melt in the microwave for 30 second bursts on medium
power until the chocolate has melted. Be careful not to
overheat the chocolate as it will burn. If the chocolate has
nearly melted but with a few lumps remaining, it is safer
to remove from the microwave and stir these lumps in to
melt them.

Place the melted chocolate, avocado, brandy and coffee
into a large mixing bowl and mix with an electric mixer on
high speed for 1 minute until the ingredients are combined.
Spread the mixture thickly over the cooled tart base. Place
in the fridge to chill and set for at least 1 hour. Once the
tart is fully chilled, melt the remaining chocolate using the
same method as before. Half dip your prunes in the melted
chocolate and place around the edge of the tart. Pop 3-5
half dipped prunes in a little mound in the centre. Sprinkle
the toasted hazelnuts over the centre of the tart.

Keeps in the fridge
for 3 days

TIP

Serve with a dairy free and vegan ice
cream and drizzle with extra melted
chocolate if you wish

Pineapple Upside Down Cake

MAKES 1 X 20CM LOOSE BOTTOMED CAKE TIN

FREE FROM GLUTEN / DAIRY

Another blast from the '70s, this is a great recipe to have up your kaftan sleeve. It's dead simple to put together and if pineapple is a bit of a faff to procure and prepare, try apple, mango or pear.

Roasted pineapple

1 pineapple, peeled, cored and sliced into rings
½ tsp ground star anise
3 tbsp honey
6 fresh cherries, pitted

Cake

2 eggs
140g crystallised sweetener of choice
70g ground almond
70g sorghum flour
25g ground golden flaxseed
1½ tsp gluten free baking powder
1 tsp vanilla paste
175ml vegetable oil, plus extra for brushing

Keeps in the fridge for 3 days. Can be frozen

TIP

Drench the cake whilst still warm with rum and/or serve with rum ice cream

Preheat the oven to 200°C / Gas 6.

Brush the cake tin with vegetable oil and place a disc of baking parchment on the bottom.

Place the pineapple in a roasting tin and sprinkle on the star anise and honey. Roast for 10 minutes. Remove from the oven, add the cherries to the roasting tin and spoon any juices over the fruits. Pop back in the oven for another 10 minutes. Set aside to cool.

Reduce the oven to 170°C / Gas 3.

To make the cake, place the eggs into a large bowl followed by the dry ingredients. Then add the vanilla paste and vegetable oil and mix with an electric mixer on high speed for approximately 1 minute, until the ingredients are combined.

Place the pineapple and cherries on the bottom of the tin, bearing in mind this will form the top of the cake. To create a pretty looking cake, position your fruit with care. Pour the cake mixture over the fruit and bake in the oven for 45 minutes or until golden brown, risen and firm to the touch. The cake may need covering with baking parchment or tin foil midway through baking if the top is browning too quickly. Leave the pudding for a couple of minutes before turning out onto a serving plate. Serve warm.

'Funky Monkey' Chocolate Cheesecake

MAKES 1 X 20CM LOOSE BOTTOMED CAKE TIN
FREE FROM GLUTEN / DAIRY

We had to be vigilant when developing this recipe as we had a steady stream of inquisitive team members, desperate to get stuck in and road test it themselves. It is a proper show stopper and tastes suitably decadent. Our team were genuinely taken aback to learn it is dairy free.

Base

225g ground hazelnuts

110ml rapeseed oil

200g Date Paste (see page 197)

85g pistachios, chopped and roasted

¼ tsp salt

100g pumpkin seeds

1 egg

85g dried cranberries

100g raisins

Roasted bananas

8 ripe bananas, peeled and cut into 1cm thick slices

2 tbsp runny honey

Filling

100ml pasteurised liquid egg white

Batch of Chocolate Banana Spread (see page 196)

Chocolate Banana Spread

Preheat the oven to 170°C / Gas 3.

Line the bottom of the cake tin with baking parchment.

Place all the base ingredients into a bowl and beat with an electric mixer on high speed for 1 minute until the ingredients are well combined. Press this mixture into the tin using the back of a metal spoon. Bake for 20 minutes or until golden brown. Leave in its tin and allow to cool.

Increase the oven to 200°C / Gas 6.

Place the bananas into a roasting tin and drizzle with the honey. Roast for 10-12 minutes or until the bananas are soft but still holding their shape without collapsing. Set to one side to cool.

For the filling, whisk the liquid egg white until stiff peaks form. Gently fold a third of the egg white at a time into the chocolate banana spread. This will make for a lighter mousse-like texture.

Place two thirds of the banana slices on top of the cheesecake base, sat up against the inside of the tin. Next, spoon the cheesecake filling into the centre of the tin and spread the mixture outwards. This will help keep the banana slices in position around the inside of the tin. Pile the remaining third of the bananas on top of the cheesecake. Any remaining syrup in the roasting tin can be drizzled over the top. Cover the tin with cling film. Leave to set in the fridge for 2-3 hours or overnight.

To serve, run a palette knife around the inside of the tin, taking care not to slice through the bananas, and remove the upper part of the loose bottomed tin. Slide a fish slice under the cheesecake to lift it up from the tin base, then peel away the baking parchment and place the cheesecake onto a plate.

Keeps in the fridge for 3 days

TIP

We found it was best to use ripe bananas as they're less likely to go black when roasted

A CAKE OF PURE BEAUTY THAT'S DELICIOUSLY FRUITY

NAISH
FARM
PYO

rhubarb rhubarb rhubarb

Rhubarb & Custard Cake

MAKES 2 X 23CM ROUND CAKES
FREE FROM GLUTEN

One of our staple puds growing up was stewed rhubarb and custard. The pick and mix sweeties of the same name were also highly prized. We wanted to convert this into another pudcake hybrid. This can be eaten on its own or with lashings of the yummy yellow stuff.

Cake

400g fresh rhubarb

350g melted butter, plus extra for brushing

280g crystallised sweetener of choice

140g ground almond

140g sorghum flour

50g ground golden flaxseed

3 tsp gluten free baking powder

2 tsp vanilla paste

2 tsp ground nutmeg

3 heaped tbsp gluten free custard powder, mixed with 3 tbsp of hot (not boiling) tap water

1 tbsp honey

4 eggs

Filling

165g double cream

70g custard

½ tsp vanilla paste

4 tbsp Rhubarb Half Jam (see page 197)

Preheat the oven to 180°C / Gas 4.

Brush the inside of the cake tins thoroughly with melted butter and line the bottoms with baking parchment.

Wash, trim and thinly slice your rhubarb. You can use the rhubarb as it is, or if you prefer less tartness, you can roast the rhubarb drizzled with runny honey for 15 minutes. Once cooked, separate off 50g for the topping and set aside.

Put the melted butter into a large mixing bowl with all the other cake ingredients except the eggs and sliced rhubarb. Beat the mixture with an electric mixer on high speed for 1 minute until smooth. Then add the eggs and mix again until smooth and well combined. Gently fold in the 350g of sliced rhubarb using a spatula.

Divide the mixture evenly between the 2 tins. Halfway through baking, cover each tin with foil to stop the cakes browning too much. Bake for 40-45 minutes until the surface of the cake is springy to the touch, and a cake skewer comes out cleanly.

Allow the cakes to cool for 5 minutes in their tins before turning them out onto a cooling rack, and leave to cool completely. Then spread 1 cake with the Rhubarb Half Jam.

For the filling, place the cream, custard and vanilla into a bowl and beat with an electric mixer on high speed for approximately 2-3 minutes. The mixture should be thick and spreadable in consistency. Spread the filling over the jammed cake and sandwich together.

For the topping take the 50g reserved roasted rhubarb and spoon in a little central mound on top of the cake.

Keeps in the fridge for 3 days

TIP

A meringue topping would bump this into posh pudding territory

FESTIVAL
FAVOURITES

Food for happy campers

Some *yummy*
recipes to inspire
you to cook
around the camp fire

Veggie Koftas with Soft Patties

MAKES 20 WALNUT SIZED KOFTAS
FREE FROM GLUTEN / DAIRY / NUTS

These Koftas are like mini veggie burgers. Baked in the oven, rather than fried. They're pretty darn virtuous.

Kofta

1 tbsp rapeseed oil, for frying

3 garlic cloves, peeled and finely chopped

3cm piece root ginger, peeled and finely grated

1 tsp crushed coriander seeds

1 tsp cumin seeds

½ tsp mustard seeds

1 fresh chilli, deseeded and finely chopped

100g peas

1 carrot, peeled and finely diced

1 head of broccoli, cut into small florets

200g tinned sweetcorn, drained

2 medium red onions, peeled and finely chopped

1 egg, beaten

100g chickpea flour, plus extra for dusting

½ tsp salt

2 tbsp fresh coriander, chopped

Grated zest of ½ a lemon

Finishing

Batch of Beetroot Tapenade
(see page 182)

Batch of Soft Patties (see page 189)

Preheat the oven to 180°C / Gas 4.

Line a baking sheet with baking parchment.

Warm the rapeseed oil in a large frying pan on a medium heat. Add the garlic, ginger, all the seeds and chilli. Cook until the garlic and ginger start to soften, which should take a couple of minutes. At the same time, crush the seeds with the back of a wooden spoon against the bottom of the pan to release their flavour. Add the vegetables and cook for a further 3-4 minutes, stirring frequently until they have started to soften.

Tip this mixture into a bowl and allow to cool. Add the egg, chickpea flour, salt, coriander and lemon zest and mix well with a spatula, until a soft dough is formed. Dust your hands with chickpea flour then roll the dough into walnut sized balls and place on the baking sheet. The dough is a bit wet but will bind together when baked.

Bake in the oven for 10-12 minutes. Once baked spread the soft patties with beetroot tapenade and sandwich 3 or 4 koftas together between 2 patties.

Eat immediately. Can be frozen

TIP Defrosted frozen peas and sweetcorn work well as does tinned sweetcorn

Apple Rings in Cider Batter

SERVES 4-6 PEOPLE
FREE FROM GLUTEN / DAIRY / NUTS

For the last 5 Octobers we've held an Apple Day at Honeybuns celebrating this humble, hard working fruit. We lay on a bit of a show with apple bobbing, apple pressing and general merriment. For refreshment there is Scrumpy on tap and platters of these most munchable of snacks. Delicious served with lashings of brandy butter or ginger ice cream.

Apple rings
6 eating apples
Rapeseed oil, for frying

Batter
100g sorghum flour
85g polenta
1 tsp cinnamon
2 eggs
200ml sparkling cider, chilled

Cinnamon sugar
2 tbsp golden icing sugar
1 tsp ground cinnamon

Preheat the oven to 200°C / Gas 6.

Line a tray with some kitchen roll.

Cut each apple horizontally in half, cut out the core sections and discard. Cut into 1½cm rings. Roast in the oven for 8 minutes. They will have turned slightly brown and slightly softened. Set aside to cool.

To make the batter, place all the ingredients into a bowl and mix well with an electric mixer on high speed for 1 minute until the ingredients are combined. Chill until required.

Sieve together the icing sugar and cinnamon and set to one side.

Preheat a small saucepan on a high heat with approximately 2cm depth of rapeseed oil. To test whether the oil is hot enough, drop a small amount of the batter into it. If it sizzles immediately, then the oil is hot enough, if not, the batter will sink. Please be careful not to leave the pan of hot oil unattended.

Dip the apple rings in the batter, ensuring they are well coated. Place the rings gently into the saucepan and turn down to a medium heat. Fry until golden brown, turning them after approximately 2-3 minutes to evenly cook. Drain on the kitchen roll, dust with cinnamon sugar and serve immediately.

Best eaten hot out of the pan

We left the skin on the apples but you can peel them if you prefer

The rolls will keep in an airtight container for 2 days. Can be frozen

TIP

To make this nut free, swap the chestnut flour for the milled flaxseed, sunflower and pumpkin seed blend

Mushroom Burgers
with Butternut Rolls

MAKES 6 ROLLS
FREE FROM GLUTEN / DAIRY

Once you have gotten the hang of the bread you can keep pre-baked rolls in the freezer. Likewise the Peasto can be prepped in advance. Equally delicious served with Charlotte's Tomato Sauce (page 194) instead of the Peasto, if you prefer.
We used a 6 cup ball pan but you can heap the dough directly onto a lined baking sheet in free form mounds instead.

Rolls

1 butternut squash, peeled and roughly chopped

4 tsp runny honey

125g sorghum flour

115g chestnut flour

40g polenta

2 tsp gluten free baking powder

1 tsp garam masala

½ tsp salt

½ tsp cracked black pepper

100ml rapeseed oil, plus extra for brushing

3 eggs

Mushrooms

6 large Portobello mushrooms, wiped clean and stem cut out

2 tbsp rapeseed oil

6 tbsp Peasto (see page 181)

Herby eggs

2 tbsp fresh herbs, finely chopped

Pinch of sea salt

Pinch of cracked black pepper

Rapeseed oil, for frying

6 free range eggs

Preheat the oven to 200°C / Gas 6.

Place the butternut squash in a roasting tin, drizzle with 2 teaspoons of honey and mix well with your hands or a metal spoon. Roast for 25 minutes, stirring halfway through the cooking time to prevent from sticking. Remove from the oven and allow to cool. Mash the butternut squash with a masher.

Reduce the oven to 180°C / Gas 4.

To make the rolls, brush a 6 cup ball pan with rapeseed oil. Place all of the dry ingredients into a mixing bowl with the mashed butternut squash, and mix in with a fork. Pour the rapeseed oil into a separate mixing bowl, add the eggs and remaining honey, and whisk until well beaten and slightly frothy. Pour this wet mixture over the dry mix. Beat with an electric mixer on high speed for 1 minute until well combined. Spoon the batter evenly into 6 dollops of dough in the ball pan. If you are making the rolls without the pan, pile up 1½ heaped dessert spoons of mixture to make 6 rustic looking mounds. Bake for 15 minutes or until a skewer comes out clean. Remove from the oven and set aside to cool completely.

Reduce the oven to 170°C / Gas 3.

Place the mushrooms cup side up on individual pieces of foil, which are big enough to wrap around the mushrooms. Place 1 teaspoon of rapeseed oil on the foil around each mushroom and at least ½ tablespoon of Peasto on the mushroom, more if you wish. Individually wrap the foils around the mushrooms and close on top to prevent any juices leaking out during cooking. Place on a baking tray in the oven for 10-12 minutes or until the mushrooms are cooked through and produce lovely juices in the foil parcel. Slice open your rolls sideways and spread each bottom half with ½ tablespoon of Peasto.

For the herby eggs, mix the chopped herbs and seasoning in a bowl. Warm 1 tablespoon rapeseed oil in a frying pan on a high heat, crack in an egg, and sprinkle a sixth of the herb and seasoning mix over the yolk before the egg fully sets. Cook a maximum of 2 eggs at a time, so you don't overcrowd the pan, adding more rapeseed oil for each egg.

Gently open the mushrooms from the foil and lift each of them onto the bottom halves of the rolls. Pour any juices from each foil back over the cup of the mushroom. When your eggs are just as you like them, lift them out and place on top of the mushrooms. Place the top half of your roll gently on top of the egg being careful not to break the yolk and devour with glee.

 Omit the sorghum flour, chestnut flour and polenta, and replace with 280g of gluten free self-raising flour. Instead of 2 teaspoons of baking powder just use 1 teaspoon.

Easy peasy pea cakes

Pea Cakes

with Cucumber & Chilli Dipping Sauce

MAKES 25-30 CANAPE CAKES
FREE FROM GLUTEN / NUTS

This recipe with the cheddar in the batter and the oriental flavours in the topping is rather contradictory but does work really well together.

Batter

125g fresh or frozen peas, cooked, cooled, and blitzed to a roughly textured pulp

100g crème fraiche

12 fresh mint leaves, chopped

100g butter, melted and cooled slightly

150ml milk

2 eggs

100g vegetarian cheddar, grated

85g polenta

75g sorghum flour

1½ tsp gluten free baking powder

½ tsp bicarbonate of soda

1 tsp cracked black pepper

½ tsp salt

Rapeseed oil, for frying

Finishing

100g crème fraiche for finishing

Batch of Cucumber & Chilli Dipping Sauce (see page 199)

Line a tray with kitchen roll.

Place all the batter ingredients except the rapeseed oil into a bowl and beat with an electric mixer on high speed for 1 minute until the ingredients are well combined.

Warm 1 tablespoon of rapeseed oil in a frying pan on a high heat. Spoon 1 heaped tablespoon of the batter into the pan and reduce to a medium heat. Allow to sizzle in the pan for 1-2 minutes, you'll need to gently lift the pea cake with a fish slice to check if the underside has turned golden brown. Once golden brown, turn it over to cook the other side. Cook no more than 3 at a time in the pan, otherwise you will lose heat. Lift onto the kitchen roll to soak up any excess oil and cover them with foil to keep warm whilst cooking the rest. Continue until you have used up all the mixture. Add rapeseed oil to the pan a little at a time as required.

To finish, place a dollop of crème fraiche on top of the pea cake then on top of that a spoonful of the Cucumber & Chilli Dipping Sauce. Alternatively, place the cakes on a big platter with a small bowl of crème fraiche together with the Cucumber & Chilli Dipping Sauce and get your guests to help themselves.

 *Omit the polenta, sorghum flour and baking powder and replace with 165g gluten free self-raising flour.*

Best eaten immediately.
Can be frozen

 TIP
This versatile mix can be baked as muffins. Butter a 12 hole muffin tin, make the batter and use 2 heaped tablespoons per muffin. Bake at 180°C / Gas 4 for 18-20 minutes instead of frying

Tortilla Wraps or Chips

MAKES 6-8 WRAPS OR ABOUT 35 CHIPS
FREE FROM GLUTEN / DAIRY / NUTS
VEGAN

This is a lovely recipe. Simplicity personified and two for the price of one. You can make beautifully soft wraps by frying off the flattened dough. For crisp chips you simply snip the soft tortilla into triangles and oven bake. You must use Masa Harina flour, easily obtainable online or at good delis/international food shops, rather than any other kind.

225g Masa Harina, plus extra for dusting

360ml hot water

½ tsp salt

Approximately 2 tbsp rapeseed oil, for brushing

Preheat the oven to 190°C / Gas 5 if making tortilla chips.

Place all the ingredients apart from the rapeseed oil into a bowl and mix together using a wooden spoon. It will take approximately 1 minute of mixing until the ingredients are fully combined.

Liberally dust a work surface with Masa Harina. Divide the dough evenly into 8 balls and then flatten them with the palm of your hand. Place 1 ball of dough at a time between 2 sheets of baking parchment. Using a rolling pin, roll over the top piece of baking parchment to flatten out the dough ball to approximately 20cm diameter.

Gently peel off the top layer of paper and you will be left with a round tortilla resting on the bottom piece of baking parchment. Repeat until you have 8 flat tortillas. The tortillas are quite fragile so you need to carefully transfer them from the baking parchment to the pan.

Brush a frying pan or wok with rapeseed oil and heat up on a high heat before adding a tortilla. Cook for 1-2 minutes on each side until you can see speckles of brown appear on the underside of the tortilla. They look similar to pancakes when ready. Continue until you have cooked them all. They are now ready to use as wraps. Set them aside to cool.

If making tortilla chips, cut the fried tortillas into triangles using scissors and bake for 7 minutes. Flip them over and bake for another 3-5 minutes until crisp.

Tortillas and chips keep in the fridge for 3 days. Can be frozen

TIP

Get creative with added seasoning. We love chilli flakes and generous amounts of chopped, fresh mint which you simply add to the dough

Lally's Salad
with Minted Wraps

MAKES 2 WRAPS
FREE FROM GLUTEN / DAIRY

This is inspired by backpacking adventures in Sri Lanka a million years ago, or so it feels. The flavours of the food we enthusiastically tried out were memorably fresh and beautifully balanced betwixt sweet and savoury.

Salad

100g peanuts, toasted

1 red chilli, finely chopped

1 tbsp lime juice

2cm piece root ginger, finely chopped

2 tbsp Satay Sauce (see page 199)

2 tbsp fresh coriander, chopped

2 tbsp dried coconut, curls or fresh

1 mango, peeled, stone removed and diced

1 tbsp honey

Wraps

2 tbsp rapeseed oil, for frying

2 eggs

2 tbsp coconut milk

1 tsp honey

2 tbsp fresh mint, finely chopped

Finely grated zest of ½ a lime

Place all the salad ingredients into a bowl and mix well.

To make the wraps, place half the rapeseed oil into a frying pan on a high heat. Whisk together the eggs, coconut milk, honey, mint and lime zest in a bowl until well combined.

Place half the mixture into the frying pan and quickly tilt the pan to ensure the egg mixture covers the whole of the bottom of the pan. Allow the mixture to set so that when you gently lift the edge it is starting to brown. You may need to reduce the heat as they burn quite quickly. Gently turn the wrap over to brown the other side. Once cooked, slide the wrap onto a plate and set to one side. Repeat this process with the other half of the mixture for the second wrap. Allow both wraps to cool completely.

To finish, spread half of your salad through the centre of each wrap, then roll up and serve.

Best eaten on the day

The mango can be substituted for nectarine if you prefer

FESTIVAL FAVES

ADULT DRINKS

Rock 'n' Roll

band tshirt

FACT OR 20

TICKETS

ADMIT ONE

BOBBLE HAT

sunnies

Tempura Vegetables

SERVES 4-6
FREE FROM GLUTEN / DAIRY / NUTS
VEGAN WITHOUT DIP

This is a lovely dish to share as an easy supper. The trick is to fry off a few at a time and serve them piping hot. The only downside is, like a BBQ or pancake session, someone needs to be on stove duty to maintain supplies.

Veg suggestions:

A total approximate weight of 800g of mixed vegetables, from the following list:

Baby corn

Peppers

Cauliflower florettes

Purple sprouting broccoli

Baby courgettes

Courgette flowers

Button mushrooms

Chantenay carrots or carrot slices

Cucumber, cut into batons

Radishes

Fennel slices

Okra

Batter

280ml sparkling water, chilled

140g rice flour, plus extra for dusting

½ tsp each salt

½ tsp cracked black pepper

Rapeseed oil, for frying

Finishing

Batch of Cucumber & Chilli Dipping Sauce (see page 199)

Line a tray with some kitchen roll.

Clean, peel and cut all the vegetables into bite size pieces. Dust them all in rice flour.

To make the batter, place all the ingredients apart from the rapeseed oil into a bowl and mix with an electric mixer on high speed for 1 minute until the ingredients are combined. Chill until required.

Preheat a small saucepan on a high heat with approximately 2cm depth of rapeseed oil. To test whether the oil is hot enough, drop a small amount of the batter into it. If it sizzles immediately then the oil is hot enough, if not, the batter will sink. Please be careful not to leave the pan of hot oil unattended. Coat a handful of the vegetables in the tempura batter, shaking off any excess, and place them carefully into the hot oil. Turn after 1 minute or so, so that the pieces cook evenly.

When the batter is crispy all over, lift the Tempura Vegetables out of the pan using tongs and place on the kitchen roll to drain. You can keep these warm by covering with foil. Keep going until you have used up all the vegetables and/or batter.

The Tempura Vegetables are best served hot and are delicious dunked into the Cucumber & Chilli Dipping Sauce.

Eat immediately

TIP

You can add chopped herbs and chilli to the batter for added oom pah pah

Mushroom Bhajis

with Raita Dip

MAKES 15 BHAJIS
FREE FROM GLUTEN / DAIRY / NUTS

This is a sociable sharing starter in its own right. Or it can form part of a mezze style feast with various dips and tapenades on hand (see page 180). Any mushrooms will work well, as you are going to shred them in the food processor so size and shape matter not a jot.

Raita dip
500g dairy free coconut yoghurt
¼ cucumber, peeled and finely chopped, or can be grated
1 tsp cracked black pepper
4 tbsp of fresh mint, chopped
3 garlic cloves, minced

Bhaji mix
125g mushrooms, wiped clean
3 spring onions, topped and tailed
2 tbsp rapeseed oil, plus extra for frying
1 tbsp cumin seeds
1 tsp fenugreek seeds
1 tsp turmeric
1 tsp ground coriander
1 tsp chilli powder or ½ fresh chilli, finely chopped
¼ tsp salt

Batter
125g chickpea flour
200ml coconut milk
2 eggs

Line a tray with some kitchen roll.

For the raita dip, place all the ingredients into a bowl and mix well with a spoon. Keep in the fridge until you are ready to serve the bhajis.

Place the mushrooms in a food processor with the spring onions and blitz for up to 1 minute; you want to keep some texture.

Warm 1 tablespoon of rapeseed oil in a frying pan on a high heat. When hot, add the cumin and fenugreek seeds. Crush them with the back of a wooden spoon against the bottom of the pan and fry for 2-3 minutes, stirring frequently. They will smell amazing and will have darkened in colour when done. Turn down to a medium heat and add an extra 1 tablespoon of rapeseed oil to the pan. Add the chopped mushrooms and spring onions to the seeds and fry for a further 3-4 minutes. The mushrooms will release juice when cooked. Towards the end of the cooking time add the rest of the spices and salt. Once cooked, remove from the heat and allow to cool slightly. Place the mushroom mixture into a sieve and gently press down to squeeze out any excess moisture. Place to one side.

To make the batter, place the chickpea flour, coconut milk and eggs into a bowl. Mix with an electric mixer on high speed for 1 minute to form a spoonable batter. Add the mushroom mixture to the batter and whizz again with the electric mixer until the ingredients are combined.

Preheat a small saucepan on a high heat with approximately 2cm depth of rapeseed oil. To test whether the oil is hot enough, drop a small amount of the bhaji mix into it. If it sizzles immediately then the oil is hot enough, if not, the batter will sink. Please be careful not to leave the pan of hot oil unattended.

Drop heaped teaspoons of mixture into the hot oil and fry until the bhajis turn golden. Flip them over halfway through cooking. They should take 2-3 minutes to cook. Place on the kitchen roll to drain.

The bhajis are best served hot and are delicious dunked into the raita dip.

Best eaten immediately. Can be frozen

TIP
You can use courgettes or your favourite veg instead of the mushrooms

Garlicky Veg with Halloumi

SERVES 2 AS A STARTER
FREE FROM GLUTEN / NUTS

This is just gorgeous. The sweet smoked paprika adds depth of flavour and the homemade oven roasted tomatoes are really worth the effort as they are much tastier than their sundried counterparts.

1 courgette

2 tbsp olive oil

5 garlic cloves

¼ tsp salt

¼ tsp cracked black pepper

150g cherry tomatoes

1 tbsp gluten free balsamic vinegar

60g marinated artichoke hearts, drained

½ tsp sweet smoked paprika (we use La Chinata)

50g Oven Roasted Tomatoes (see page 195)

3 tbsp of fresh coriander, chopped

150g vegetarian halloumi, cut into 1cm cubes

Preheat the oven to 200°C / Gas 6.

Roughly chop the courgette into chunks of about 2cm wide and pop into a roasting tin. Add 1 tablespoon of olive oil, the garlic, salt and pepper, and stir well. Roast for 20–25 minutes, until the courgette has started to brown.

Place the cherry tomatoes in a roasting tin along with the balsamic vinegar and 1 tablespoon of olive oil. Stir well and roast in the oven for 10-15 minutes, at the same time as the courgette. Remove both trays from the oven and leave to cool.

Reserve half of the roasted courgette chunks, then pop the rest into a food processor along with the artichoke, paprika, Oven Roasted Tomatoes, roasted cherry tomatoes and coriander. Don't blitz for more than 1 minute, as you want to retain some texture.

Fry the halloumi cubes in a pan for 3-4 minutes on each side, until golden brown. Allow to cool.

Spoon the blitzed dip into a serving dish and either stir in the remaining courgette and halloumi or place decoratively over the top to serve.

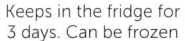

Keeps in the fridge for 3 days. Can be frozen

TIP
This recipe works brilliantly as a topping for the Farinata bread (see page 193)

Best Dhal

SERVES 6 AS A SIDE OR 4 AS A MAIN
FREE FROM GLUTEN / DAIRY / NUTS
VEGAN

This was inspired by a lovely lemon dhal soup served at our dependably excellent local curry house, The India Cottage in Henstridge... it's worth a cheeky visit if you're ever in our neck of the woods.

Roasted vegetables

2 red peppers, deseeded and chopped

2 red onions, peeled and roughly chopped

1 red chilli, deseeded and finely chopped

2 garlic cloves, peeled and finely chopped

Dhal

150g split red lentils

400ml coconut milk

½ tsp toasted cumin seeds

¼ tsp salt, or to taste

200ml water

1 tsp coriander seeds, toasted

Finely grated zest and juice of 1 lemon

Preheat the oven to 200°C / Gas 6.

Place all the vegetables in a roasting tin and cook for 20 minutes, or until they start to darken at the edges.

Place the lentils in a thick bottomed saucepan with the coconut milk, cumin seeds and salt. Swill out the coconut milk tin with the water and add to the pan. Bring to the boil, then turn down to simmer for 15-20 minutes, stirring regularly. The Dhal will thicken and the liquid will reduce. Taste the lentils to ensure that they are fully softened.

When cooked, remove from the heat and add the coriander seeds, lemon zest and juice and roasted vegetables. Mix in with a wooden spoon.

Tip into a serving dish and serve immediately.

Keeps in the fridge for
3 days. Can be frozen

TIP

This is utterly delicious with or
without the roasted vegetables

![Fruit Coolers photo]

Fruit Coolers

**MAKES 10 ICE LOLLIES
(USING STANDARD MOULDS)
FREE FROM GLUTEN / DAIRY / NUTS
VEGAN**

We just selected the fruit we fancied, but feel free to use what you wish. Other fruits worth trying are strawberry, peach and blackcurrant with a slug of liquor if the kiddlers have gone to bed.

250ml coconut cream

6 mint leaves

2 mangoes, peeled and diced

½ tsp vanilla paste

Batch of Raspberry Pesto (see page 181)

Blitz all the ingredients thoroughly in a food processor for up to 2 minutes. Pour into your lolly moulds and freeze overnight.

Keep frozen

TIP

As shown in our photo, you can use an ice cube tray instead of lolly moulds

Yum

Carrot Flips

with Coconut Milk Ice

MAKES 20 SMALL FLIPS
FREE FROM GLUTEN / DAIRY / NUTS

These lovely little bites were inspired by a carrot cake we used to make. We were intrigued by the idea of crossing a cake with a pancake and therefore negating the need to switch the oven on. Cheaty in a good way.

Batter

2 small carrots, grated

50g polenta

35g tapioca flour

25g sorghum flour

40g crystallised sweetener of choice

75ml soya or coconut milk

100ml unrefined coconut oil

2 eggs

Finely grated zest of 1 small orange

½ tsp mixed spice

40g sultanas

1 tsp gluten free baking powder

½ tsp salt

Rapeseed oil, for frying

Finishing

Batch of Coconut Milk Ice (see page 198)

Place all the batter ingredients into a bowl and beat with an electric mixer on high speed for 1 minute until smooth.

Warm 1 tablespoon of rapeseed oil in a non-stick frying pan on a high heat. Spoon 1 heaped tablespoon of batter into the pan and reduce to a medium heat. Allow to sizzle in the pan for 1-2 minutes; you'll need to gently lift the carrot flip up with a fish slice to check if the underside has turned golden brown. Once golden brown, turn it over to cook the other side. Cook no more than 3 at a time in the pan, otherwise you will lose heat. Tip them onto a serving plate and cover with foil to keep warm whilst cooking the rest. Add rapeseed oil to the pan a little as a time, as required.

Place 3-4 carrot flips onto each plate, and scoop the Coconut Milk Ice on top.

Best eaten hot out of the pan

TIP

If you do want to bake rather than fry, this mixture will make 6 muffins. Bake at 170°C / Gas 3 for 12 minutes

flip me

THE PERFECT REASON
TO USE UP THOSE
RIPE BANANAS

Eggy Banana Bread Sandwiches

1 X 900G LOAF TIN, MAKES 6 SANDWICHES
FREE FROM GLUTEN / DAIRY / NUTS

*This is a wonderful mid morning pick me up after
a night of festival frivolity.*

Banana Bread

75ml rapeseed oil, plus extra for brushing

2 eggs

100g runny honey

50g sorghum flour

100g milled flaxseed, sunflower and pumpkin seed blend

1 tsp ground cinnamon

½ tsp ground star anise

1 tsp gluten free baking powder

½ tsp bicarbonate of soda

60g pumpkin seeds, roughly chopped and
toasted, plus 15g extra for the top of the loaf

35g sunflower seeds, toasted

325g ripe banana slices (peeled weight),
approximately 1cm width slices

Spread

Batch of Chocolate Banana Spread (see page 196)

Eggy mix

1 egg

½ tsp vanilla paste

50ml coconut milk

2 tbsp rapeseed oil, for frying

Preheat the oven to 170°C / Gas 3.

Line the loaf tin with baking parchment and brush the paper
with rapeseed oil.

Place all the banana bread ingredients, apart from the
banana, into a large bowl and beat with an electric mixer
on high speed for 1 minute. Add the banana slices and
stir in with a spoon. Pour the mixture into the prepared
tin. Sprinkle the top with your remaining toasted pumpkin
seeds. Place in the oven for 35-40 minutes until springy
to the touch. Leave the loaf to cool completely before
removing from the tin.

Carefully cut the banana bread into 12 slices. It is quite
delicate. Spread half the slices thickly with the Chocolate
Banana Spread, then sandwich together with the remaining
slices to form 6 sandwiches, pressing gently to ensure they
are stuck together.

To make the eggy mix, place the egg, vanilla and coconut
milk in a bowl and whisk for 1-2 minutes until the ingredients
are combined.

Warm 2 tablespoons of rapeseed oil in a frying pan on a
high heat. Dip each of the prepared sandwiches into the
eggy mix, making sure to coat both sides.

Place a sandwich at a time into the hot pan (it should sizzle
straight away), and fry for 2-3 minutes on each side until
golden brown.

*Replace the sorghum flour and milled seed
blend with 150g gluten free self-raising flour.*

Flour swap

PERFECT
WITH A CUPPA

The banana bread keeps
in the fridge for 3 days.
Can be frozen

TIP

Roasted butternut squash
works well instead of the bananas

CRACKERS, DIPS & FLAVOUR BLENDS

A bit of that
and a jar of this,
mix it all together
for some foody bliss

PESTOS &

TAPENADES

Here is a collection of flavour packed, super simple tapenades and pestos which can all be whizzed up in a couple of minutes.

We've departed from the traditional definitions of pesto and tapenade by embracing different combinations of vegetables and herbs, and even fruit such as our Raspberry Pesto for desserts. Pestos tend to be runnier in consistency than tapenades, which are often chunkier, but both have similar uses. You can add more or less olive oil to change the consistency for different uses, e.g. add more oil to make a "drizzle-able" sauce or dressing. We've used seeds to make this selection nut free, but you can always add in toasted pistachios, almonds or hazelnuts if you have them to hand. Have a rummage through your store cupboard and get creative with the flavours.

Each recipe makes 1 small bowl.

All these dips store in sterilised jars. Keep in the fridge for 5 days. Can be frozen.

SERVING SUGGESTIONS FOR THE SAVOURY PESTOS AND TAPENADES:

STIR INTO A LASAGNE, MOUSAKKA OR SOUP FOR EXTRA FLAVOUR

MIX IN WITH PASTA OR RICE

SPREAD ON TOAST OR ON A PIZZA BASE

SERVE WITH CRACKERS AND CRUDITÉS (SEE PAGES 187)

MAKE A FLAVOURSOME MASHED POTATO

USE INSTEAD OF CHUTNEY WITH A CHEESEBOARD

FILL TART CASES AND LAYER UP WITH OTHER INGREDIENTS

Peasto

**FREE FROM GLUTEN / DAIRY / NUTS
VEGAN**

150g peas, fresh or frozen, brought to the boil and drained

10 fresh mint leaves

8 fresh basil leaves

¼ tsp salt

¼ tsp ground white pepper

50ml olive oil

25g pine nuts, toasted

2 garlic cloves, minced or crushed

Place all the ingredients in a food processor and blitz for 1 minute to make a smooth paste. You'll then need to scrape down the sides of the bowl and blitz for a further 30 seconds. The 50ml of olive oil in this recipe creates a great dip consistency. For a runnier pesto, add more oil. Decant into a bowl.

Raspberry Pesto

**FREE FROM GLUTEN / DAIRY / NUTS
VEGAN**

200g raspberries

25g pine nuts, toasted

12 mint leaves

2 tbsp liquid sweetener of choice (maple syrup works well)

Place all the ingredients in a food processor and blitz for 1 minute to make a smooth paste. You'll then need to scrape down the sides of the bowl and blitz for a further 30 seconds. Decant into a bowl.

FREE FROM GLUTEN / DAIRY / NUTS
VEGAN

300g gluten free pre-cooked beetroot

12 fresh mint leaves

¼ fresh fennel bulb, diced

1 tbsp maple syrup

1 tsp cracked black pepper

Place all the ingredients in a food processor and blitz. You are aiming for a chunky consistency rather than a smooth paste.

If you want to loosen the mixture up you can add olive oil, a drizzle at a time. Decant into a bowl.

FREE FROM GLUTEN / DAIRY / NUTS
VEGAN

4 tbsp fresh coriander, finely chopped

8 fresh mint leaves, finely chopped

125g black olives, pitted (we favour Kalamata)

3 tbsp wild garlic leaves, if available

1 garlic clove (2 large cloves if not using wild garlic leaves), minced or crushed

2 tbsp virgin olive oil

Juice of ½ a lemon

1 small red onion, chopped

Place all the ingredients in a food processor and blitz for 30 seconds. Scrape down the sides of the bowl and blitz for a further 30 seconds. You are aiming for a chunky consistency rather than a smooth paste. Decant into a bowl.

Tomato, Red Pepper & Pumpkin Seed Tapenade

Red Pepper & Butter Bean Tapenade

FREE FROM GLUTEN / DAIRY / NUTS
VEGAN

75g red pepper, roasted

50g Oven Roasted Tomatoes (see page 195)

25g pumpkin seeds, chopped and toasted

½ tsp cracked black pepper

2 garlic cloves, chopped and roasted

Olive oil, optional

Place all the ingredients in a food processor and blitz. You are aiming for a chunky consistency rather than a smooth paste.

If you want to loosen the mixture up you can add olive oil, a drizzle at a time. Decant into a bowl.

FREE FROM GLUTEN / DAIRY / NUTS
VEGAN

2 red peppers, deseeded and chopped

3 garlic cloves, minced

2 tbsp rapeseed oil

2 tsp fresh thyme, chopped

Squeeze of lemon juice

200g tinned butter beans, drained

2 tbsp tahini

1 tsp cracked black pepper

10 fresh oregano leaves

Preheat the oven to 180°C / Gas 4.

Drizzle the red peppers and garlic with rapeseed oil and roast for 20-25 minutes, until the pepper has just started to turn brown around the edges. Allow to cool.

Place all the ingredients in a food processor and blitz. You are aiming for a chunky consistency rather than a smooth paste. Decant into a bowl.

FLAVOUR

BLENDS

These recipes are veritable time savers. They can be pre-assembled and stored, ready to go.

Spices are prone to losing their flavour over time, so freezing them is a good storage option.

Store in airtight sterilised jars away from direct sunlight for up to 28 days, or freeze in sandwich style bags.

The Florentine Mix keeps for 2 weeks and can be frozen.

SERVING SUGGESTIONS:

DUKKAH SPICE...

ADD TO BREADS, CRACKERS AND PIZZA BASES

CHAI SPICE...

ADD TO ICE CREAM, CAKES, BISCUITS, HOT DRINKS, PORRIDGE, BREAD AND CRACKER MIXES

FLORENTINE MIX...

GREAT IN ICE CREAM, CAKES, BISCUITS, PORRIDGE AND MUESLI

Dukkah Spice

MAKES 150G
FREE FROM GLUTEN / DAIRY / NUTS
VEGAN

50g pumpkin seeds

50g sunflower seeds

25g pine nuts

2 tsp cumin seeds

2 tsp coriander seeds

¼ tsp salt

½ tsp cracked black pepper

1-2 tsp chilli flakes, depending on how hot you like it

½ tsp cinnamon

Place all the ingredients on a baking sheet and roast for approximately 5 minutes or until lightly golden. Shake the tray halfway through to help them toast evenly. Allow to cool slightly then blitz lightly in a food processor. You do not want to grind the seeds down too finely; a slight coarseness is good.

Chai Spice

MAKES 25G
FREE FROM GLUTEN / DAIRY / NUTS
VEGAN

4 tsp ground cinnamon

2 tsp ground ginger

1 tsp ground cloves

¼ tsp ground nutmeg

¼ tsp cracked black pepper

1 tsp ground cardamom

½ tsp ground star anise

Mix the ingredients together and that's it!

SEEDY FRUITY YUMMY

Florentine Mix

MAKES 200G
FREE FROM GLUTEN / DAIRY / NUTS
VEGAN

½ tsp sea salt

25g pumpkin seeds

25g sunflower seeds

1 tsp fennel seeds

25g pine nuts

1½ tsp orange oil

55g naturally coloured glacé cherries

50g dried cranberries

25g mixed peel

Preheat the oven to 200°C / Gas 6.

Spread the salt, seeds and pine nuts onto a baking sheet. Sprinkle the orange oil over the top.

To toast, pop in the oven for 6 minutes or until lightly golden. Leave to cool.

Pop the cherries, cranberries, and mixed peel into a mixing bowl and add the toasted seeds. Stir to combine all the ingredients. Tip this mixture onto a board and roughly chop using a large knife. The idea is to create slightly smaller bits but keep things looking rustic with plenty of texture.

BAKED BITS

Here's introducing a family of hardworking supporting acts, as referenced in some of our other recipes. Each recipe is versatile, and can be adapted according to the spices and herbs *you* have available. For example, the Coriander Dippers would work just as well with fresh mint or basil.

Coriander Dippers

MAKES 28 - 30 DIPPERS
FREE FROM GLUTEN / DAIRY

These are packed to the rafters with fresh herbage. Delicious eaten solo or dunked into homemade houmous or any of our dips (see page 178).

2 tbsp rapeseed oil, plus extra for brushing

125g tapioca flour, plus extra for dusting

70g ground almonds

¼ tsp gluten free baking powder

2 egg whites

4 tsp coriander seeds, toasted and crushed

3 tbsp fresh coriander leaves, finely chopped

4 garlic cloves, finely chopped

Preheat the oven to 180°C / Gas 4.

Brush 2 sheets of baking parchment with rapeseed oil.

Place all the ingredients in a food processor and blitz for 1-2 minutes until a dough is formed.

Liberally dust your hands with tapioca flour, and place the dough on the oiled side of 1 of the sheets of baking parchment. Place the second sheet (oiled face down) onto the dough. Roll the dough out as thinly as you can manage, 2mm thickness is ideal. Aim for a rough square in shape, about 30 x 30cm. Peel off the top layer of the baking parchment and transfer the bottom sheet of paper, complete with rolled out dough, onto a baking sheet.

With a sharp knife, score the dough into rectangles. You can choose what size you want your dippers to be. There is no need to cut right through the dough.

Bake for 12-15 minutes until the dippers just start to turn golden around the edges. Leave them to cool on the sheet. Once cooled, break the strips up along the knife cuts either by snapping them or running a knife back along the score lines.

Keeps in the fridge for 3 days. Can be frozen

This dough makes a lovely pizza base; just roll out thicker and increase the baking time

Lemony Croutons

MAKES 60 CROUTONS
FREE FROM GLUTEN / NUTS

We created these to accompany our Pea, Nettle & Mint Soup (see page 53) and Sprouting Super Salad (see page 129) but they can be sprinkled over many savoury dishes where a flavoursome crunch is called for.

Dry

2 tsp gluten free baking powder

100g polenta

55g sorghum flour

55g tapioca flour

3 tsp fresh thyme, chopped

¼ tsp salt

1 tsp cracked black pepper

50g grated vegetarian Italian hard cheese, grated

Wet

40g butter

150ml milk

1 tsp lemon oil

To fry

½ tbsp rapeseed oil

2 tsp Lemon & Garlic Paste (see page 195)
or use a shop bought garlic paste

Preheat the oven to 180°C / Gas 4.

Line a baking sheet with baking parchment.

Add all of the dry ingredients to a bowl, taking care to cover the baking powder.

Melt the butter in the microwave and set aside to cool a little.

Place the milk and lemon oil into a jug and beat together with a whisk. Pour this over the dry ingredients and stir well with a spatula, making sure it's all combined and smooth. Then add the melted butter and stir it in until well mixed.

Spread the mixture out onto the baking sheet using a palette knife, to approximately 2cm in thickness. Don't worry about spreading it out too evenly as the croutons look great if they're a little rustic.

Bake for 30 minutes or until golden brown. Allow to cool.

Cut up into chunks approximately 1.5 x 1.5cm. Warm the rapeseed oil in a frying pan on a high heat. Add the Lemon & Garlic Paste and turn down to a medium heat. Add the croutons, approximately a dozen at a time so as not to overcrowd the pan. Keep them moving with a fish slice and fry until golden brown and crunchy all over. This will take around 5-6 minutes.

You can serve the croutons warm or cold with your dish of choice.

Keeps in an airtight container for 7 days. Can be frozen

TIP

Try chilli oil as a change from lemon

Cheesy Nibbles

MAKES 30-35 NIBBLES
FREE FROM GLUTEN / NUTS

These delightful little morsels are perfect to serve with drinks, unadorned. Alternatively, you can use them as canapé bases - try spreading them with Peasto (page 181) and topping with vegetarian mozzarella and fresh basil leaves.

Dough

100g butter, chilled and cubed
75g milled flaxseed, sunflower and pumpkin seed blend
75g sorghum flour, plus extra for dusting
75g vegetarian mature cheddar, grated
½ tsp cracked black pepper
50ml milk

Topping

35g vegetarian mature cheddar, grated

Preheat the oven to 180°C / Gas 4.

Line a baking sheet with baking parchment.

Place all of the dough ingredients, except the milk, in a food processor and blitz until it resembles soft, clumpy breadcrumbs. Add the milk and blitz again until a dough is formed. Use straight away, do not be tempted to chill it first as it makes it very hard to roll out.

Dust your hands, rolling pin and work surface liberally with sorghum flour, and roll out the dough to approximately 5mm thickness. Cut the Cheesy Nibbles out using a small round 4cm metal cookie cutter. Using a fish slice transfer each Nibble onto the lined baking sheet. Space them out evenly to allow room for spreading. Sprinkle with the grated cheddar topping.

Bake for 8-9 minutes until they are just turning golden underneath. Serve warm or allow to cool completely on a wire rack.

Keeps in an airtight container for 5 days. Can be frozen

TIP

Sprinkle some of the Cheesy Nibbles with black onion seeds before baking

Soft Patties

MAKES 8 PATTIES
FREE FROM GLUTEN / DAIRY
VEGAN

This is a beautifully soft bread which can be used to sandwich together bhajis, koftas or falafel. The ground almonds create an almost juicy bread, full of moisture.

350g ground almonds
1 tsp salt
1 tsp gluten free baking powder
80ml rapeseed oil
235ml warm water
1 tsp sweet smoked paprika
Gluten free flour, for dusting

Preheat the oven to 170°C / Gas 3.

Line a baking sheet with baking parchment.

Place all the ingredients into a food processor and blitz until a sticky dough is formed. This will take approximately 1 minute. Using a spatula, gather up any dough from the sides of the bowl and blitz again for 30 seconds. Let the dough rest for 10 minutes; this makes the dough a little easier to handle.

Liberally dust your hands and work surface with a gluten free flour. Divide the dough into 8 balls, weighing roughly 75g each.

Roll the balls of dough in the gluten free flour and press each ball in the palm of your hand to create an oval shape, approximately 2cm thick.

Place the patties, evenly spaced, on the baking sheet. Bake for 18-22 minutes until they are firm to the touch and have turned slightly golden at the edges. Serve warm or cold.

Keeps in an airtight container for 2 days. Can be frozen

TIP

Try adding chopped Oven Roasted Tomatoes (see page 195) to the dough

Farinata

Waldorfey Salad

Cucumber, Feta & Lemon Salad

Edible flowers

Tomato, Red Pepper & Pumpkin Seed Tapenade

Beetroot Tapenade

Asparagus & Watercress Frittata

FOOD
TASTES BETTER
WITH FRIENDS

Sprouting Super Salad

Assorted Crackers

Kirsteen's Crackers

MAKES 30 CRACKERS
FREE FROM GLUTEN / DAIRY / NUTS
VEGAN

This recipe was shared with me by talented cook, Kirsteen from Canada. We've used cooked brown rice but you can go halves with cooked rice and cooked quinoa flakes if you prefer. It helps to overcook the rice just by a minute or two, to gain a mushier texture which helps when rolling the cracker dough out. Naturally, you can run amok by adding herbs and spices as you wish.

185g brown rice

25g chia seeds

25g sesame seeds

25g flax seeds

½ tsp salt

Preheat the oven to 180°C / Gas 4.

Cook the rice as per the instructions on the pack. You will need to work quickly whilst the rice is still warm to get it to blend properly.

In a food processor blitz the warm, cooked rice until it is mushy in texture. This will take approximately 1 minute. If your rice has cooled and stiffened, you can add a couple of teaspoons of hot water to loosen it up again. Add the seeds and salt. Blitz again until you have a mushy ball of dough.

Spoon half the dough onto a sheet of baking parchment and flatten it out a bit with a spoon. Cover with another piece of baking parchment. With a rolling pin, flatten the dough and roll it as thin as you can get it without it breaking up. Carefully peel the top layer of paper off and transfer the lower sheet with the rolled dough onto a baking sheet.

Repeat with the second ball of dough. You'll end up with 2 sheets of rolled cracker dough on 2 lined baking sheets.

Place both the sheets in the oven for 12-15 minutes.

Remove from the oven and carefully turn the cracker dough over, place it back on the parchment. Return to the oven for 8-10 minutes. They are ready when the edges start to catch and turn golden brown. Check the middle of the dough; if it's soft, return to the oven for 2-3 minutes.

Once completely cooled, you can break the sheets into shards to make the crackers.

Keeps in an airtight container for 5 days. Can be frozen

TIP

Instead of salt, you can try adding Welshman's Caviar (dried seaweed) instead. Try beachfood.co.uk

Farinata

MAKES 1 X 20CM LOOSE BOTTOMED CAKE TIN

FREE FROM GLUTEN / DAIRY / NUTS

This versatile bread is our take on the traditional chickpea flour bread hailing from the Mediterranean. Serve with soup, toast it, use it as a pizza base. Whatever takes your fancy.

Farinata

150ml rapeseed oil, plus extra for brushing

85g polenta

75g sorghum flour

60g chickpea flour

2½ tsp gluten free baking powder

½ tsp salt

2 eggs

150ml coconut milk

Herbs and veggies

1 tsp black onion seeds

50g capers, chopped

35g black olives, pitted and chopped

Handful of fresh basil leaves, torn

115g roasted red onion, finely chopped

Preheat the oven to 170°C / Gas 3.

Brush the cake tin with rapeseed oil.

Place all of the Farinata ingredients into a bowl and mix well with an electric mixer on high speed for 1 minute. Next, add the herbs and veggies, stirring in gently using a spatula. Pour the batter into your tin, spreading it out with a palette knife.

Bake in the oven for 15-18 minutes until golden brown. Remove from the tin and serve immediately.

 Omit the polenta, sorghum flour, chickpea flour and baking powder and replace with 225g gluten free self-raising flour.

 Best eaten on the day. Can be frozen

 TIP Substitute the roasted red onion for grated halloumi for a cheesy alternative

OTHER BITS

We have here a collection of sweet and savoury kitchen cupboard superstars.

From the easy peasy Half Jams to the flavour packed Lemon & Garlic Paste, these recipes are hugely versatile and feature in recipes throughout this book. Most recipes can be stored in the fridge and frozen.

Charlotte's Tomato Sauce

FREE FROM GLUTEN / DAIRY / NUTS VEGAN

This is a full flavoured, sugar free alternative to shop bought pasta sauces. Use with rice, added to soups, or as a dip. Try adding chopped fresh oregano, thyme and/or basil if you have them to hand.

1 tsp black onion seeds

1 tsp mustard seeds

1 tbsp rapeseed oil

1 red onion, finely chopped

150g Oven Roasted Tomatoes (see page 195), roughly chopped, or sun dried tomatoes

1 tbsp gluten free balsamic vinegar

1 tsp tomato puree

150ml-200ml water

½ tsp salt

½ tsp cracked black pepper

Add the black onion seeds and mustard seeds to a saucepan on a medium heat. Dry fry for 2 minutes, crushing the seeds against the pan with a back of a wooden spoon to release their flavour. Add the rapeseed oil to the pan together with the onion and tomatoes. Fry until the onions are just starting to brown; this will take 4-5 minutes. Add all the other ingredients and simmer on a low heat for approximately 15 minutes, stirring occasionally.

Set aside and allow to cool. Best made ahead of time and chilled for a couple of days; this allows the flavours to mingle.

 Keeps in the fridge for 5 days. Can be frozen

 TIP For posh beans on toast, add some tinned beans to the sauce and serve with toasted Farinata (see page 193)

Oven Roasted Tomatoes

**FREE FROM GLUTEN / DAIRY / NUTS
VEGAN**

*These homemade versions knock the spots
off sun dried versions... in our humble opinion
only, of course. The gentle roasting on a low
heat means they retain some moisture whilst
intensifying their flavour. They can be added to
salads, sauces or blitzed and added to dips. With
the oven on for so long, it pays to make a couple
of batches.*

500g cherry or baby plum tomatoes, halved

6 garlic cloves, thinly sliced

2 tbsp gluten free balsamic vinegar

4 tbsp of olive oil, plus extra for storing

1 tsp cracked black pepper

4 tsp fresh thyme, finely chopped

Preheat the oven to 100°C / Gas ¼.

Place all the ingredients in a roasting tin. Tumble
them together so the tomatoes are fully coated.
Roast for 1 hour 30 minutes until the tomatoes
shrink in their skins and start to caramelise at
the edges.

Once cooled completely, place into a sterilised,
lidded jar, adding extra olive oil to cover all
the tomatoes.

Keeps in a lidded jar in the
fridge for 10 days.
Can be frozen

TIP

Try red peppers as a
change from tomato

Lemon & Garlic Paste

**FREE FROM GLUTEN / DAIRY / NUTS
VEGAN**

*This is a potent mixture of full on flavours. Use
sparingly to great effect in soups, bread mixes,
savoury sauces or smeared on toast for an
intense garlic hit.*

1 whole garlic bulb, peeled and minced

Finely grated zest and juice of 2 lemons

4 tbsp olive oil

1 large sprig of fresh rosemary, leaves removed
and finely chopped

25g pine nuts, toasted and crushed

Preheat the oven to 200°C / Gas 6.

Place all the ingredients, except the toasted pine
nuts, into a bowl and mix together. Place the
mixture on a square piece of tin foil. Make a parcel
with the foil so that none of the contents can leak
out, then place on a baking sheet. Roast in the
oven for 30 minutes. Allow to cool slightly before
you open the parcel as the contents get very hot.

Place the cooled ingredients and the toasted pine
nuts into a food processor and blitz until a paste is
formed. You may need to scrape down the sides
of the bowl and blitz again.

Place into a sterilised, lidded jar and store in the
fridge until required.

Keeps in a lidded jar in
the fridge for 10 days.
Can be frozen

TIP

For another added flavour try
roasting ¼ bulb of fennel with
the rest of the ingredients

Chocolate Banana Spread

MAKES 1 LARGE BOWL OR 18-20 TRUFFLES
FREE FROM GLUTEN / DAIRY / NUTS
VEGAN

This is as nutritious as it is delicious. Try it spread on toast, as a dip, or in a cheesecake.

200g dairy free dark chocolate

20g pumpkin seeds, toasted

20g sunflower seeds, toasted

20g pine nuts or shelled hemp

1 ripe banana, mashed with a fork

125g tub dairy free and vegan coconut yoghurt

Place the chocolate in a microwaveable bowl and melt in the microwave for 30 second bursts on medium power until the chocolate has melted. Be careful not to overheat the chocolate as it will burn. If the chocolate has nearly melted but with a few lumps remaining, it is safer to remove from the microwave and stir these lumps in to melt them. Place the melted chocolate in a food processor with the other ingredients and blitz until a smooth paste is formed.

Keeps in the fridge for 5 days

TIP

To make 18-20 truffles, chill for at least 1 hour before rolling them out. Roll the mix into 20g truffles and dip in gluten free, dairy free and vegan cocoa powder. For an uber decadent treat, try a cheeky splash of rum

Half Jams

MAKES 1 JAR FULL
FREE FROM GLUTEN / DAIRY / NUTS
VEGAN

So called as they take half the time and half the hassle to make as normal jam. They also contain a smidgen of added sugar compared to their shop bought counterparts. Runnier than a regular jam and packed to the rafters with flavour.

200g fresh raspberries, blackcurrants or rhubarb

2 tbsp liquid sweetener of choice, more to taste with tart fruit

A good squeeze of lemon juice

1 tbsp cornflour mixed with 2 tbsp cold water, to make a paste

Place the fruit in a pan with the liquid sweetener and lemon juice. On a medium heat, stir the fruit until it softens and starts to split up, this will take 5-8 minutes. Remove from the heat and mash the fruit in the pan using a potato masher. Whisk the cornflour paste quickly into the mixture until it is dissolved and then return to a medium heat and stir continuously for 2-3 minutes until the jam thickens up. Allow to cool.

Keeps in a lidded jar in the fridge for 14 days. Can be frozen

TIP
These make excellent tart fillings or try spooning over porridge or Bircher

Fruit Pastes

MAKES A SMALL JAR FULL
FREE FROM GLUTEN / DAIRY / NUTS
VEGAN

You can take your pick of pretty much any dried fruit to make up a paste free from refined sugars. We use them as substitutes for sugar in some baked recipes. See page 141 for our Low Rise Rhubarb & Ginger Cheesecake.

Dates / prunes / dried apricot / raisins / dried cranberries / dried figs

Water (for every 100g of fruit you will need 1 tbsp of water)

Simply blitz your chosen dried fruit and water in a food processor until you end up with a smooth paste.

Keeps in the fridge for 5 days. Can be frozen

TIP
Date paste with added natural caramel flavour makes an excellent substitute for dulce de leche

Coconut Milk Ice

SERVES 2
FREE FROM GLUTEN / DAIRY / NUTS
VEGAN

This is a doddle to make and can be customised ad infinitum. For a touch of spice try adding a smidgen of ground and chopped crystallised ginger.

200ml coconut milk
4 tbsp coconut cream
50g coconut sugar or crystallised sweetener of choice

Place a metal bowl in the freezer for 30 minutes before you start.

Place the coconut milk and coconut cream together in the chilled metal bowl. Use an electric whisk on high speed to whip the ingredients until they thicken; this may take up to 4-5 minutes. Add the coconut sugar or crystallised sweetener and mix again for 2 minutes until the ingredients are combined and you've reached maximum thickness. Cover the bowl with foil or cling film and freeze for at least 2 hours.

Keep frozen

TIP

For a grown up treat try adding Boozy Cherries (see page 147)

Cucumber & Chilli Dipping Sauce

SERVES 4
FREE FROM GLUTEN / DAIRY / NUTS

We like this hot and use half a finely chopped chilli but if you're not sure add a little chilli at a time to taste. The aim is for the cucumber to be as finely diced as you can manage. Lovely spooned over savoury muffins or used as a dip with the Tempura Vegetables (see page 169).

¼ - ½ small red chilli, finely chopped

¼ cucumber, finely diced, and peeled if you prefer

2 tbsp mirin wine (rice wine)

1 tbsp sesame seeds, toasted

3 tbsp honey

1½ tbsp gluten free dark soy sauce

2 tbsp toasted sesame oil

1 garlic clove, finely chopped or minced

2 tbsp fresh coriander or mint, finely chopped

Place all the ingredients in a bowl and mix together with a spoon.

Best left in the fridge for at least 2 hours. This will ensure the flavours start to mingle.

Keeps in the fridge for 3 days

TIP

If you make it the day before and leave it overnight the cucumber will absorb a lot of the juice. You can use the flavour infused cucumber in Asian salads or a stir fry

Satay Sauce

SERVES 4 AS A DIP
FREE FROM GLUTEN / DAIRY
VEGAN

This is a lovely, robustly flavoured satay. We've kept the sweetness level on the low side, so you can always add a little more muscovado if you wish. Delicious served with the Coriander Dippers (see page 187).

175g peanuts, toasted

2 tbsp roasted buckwheat

2 garlic cloves, minced

1 tsp gluten free dark soy sauce

2 tsp sesame oil

2 tbsp light muscovado sugar

½ - 1 tsp chilli powder, to taste

80ml coconut milk

½ tsp tamarind paste or lime juice

Place all the ingredients in a food processor and blitz for up to 1 minute. You are aiming for a chunky textured paste. You may need to scrape down the sides of the bowl and blitz for a further 30 seconds.

Keeps in the fridge for 5 days. Can be frozen

TIP

Try adding in some toasted pistachios in place of some of the peanuts

INDEX

And now it's time to say goodbye...